Story as Theology

By Rev. Dr. Adam Navis

ii

Preface

I have always been more moved—and to more lasting effect—by stories than by the sub-genres of non-fiction, including sermons, biblical commentary, philosophical argument, or self-help. I had this gut feeling that Christians should take stories more seriously, but I couldn't articulate to my satisfaction why I felt this way. I wanted to know why stories capture our imagination. What does it mean to call a story a *Christian* story? And perhaps most importantly, how can we, as individuals and the Church, learn to tell better stories?

I began by studying the writing process. I compared popular Christian writers with students and faculty at Western Theological Seminary in order to understand the habits, attitudes, and beliefs of good Christian writers. Then I sought a way to develop these characteristics in other people. I did this by marrying the writing pedagogy of Peter Elbow with traditional Christian spiritual disciplines to create an explicitly Christian writing process. Only then did I move on to address the rhetorical, psychological, social, and theological aspects (and advantages) of the story form.

Yet the final, most important, and most vulnerable step was to put it all into practice: to write a story about what it means to be a Christian and a writer. This was not secondary or merely illustrative, but the inevitable conclusion of my work. After all, it would be ironic and hypocritical to celebrate the form of the story and then neglect to use its power.

Contents

Introduction:

A Storytelling Renaissance

If you were looking for a new podcast in the summer of 2014, you probably heard about *Serial*. The series told the story of Syed Adnan, who was convicted of the murder of his ex-girlfriend Hae Min Lee while they were both still in high school. It was such a phenomena that you didn't need to go to iTunes' "most popular" podcast list to find it. You could just as easily hear about it on Facebook, Twitter, or directly from a zealous friend.

What set *Serial* apart from other story-based programs was that the producers wanted to attempt long-form storytelling. They wanted to *serialize* a single story. This was counter to perceived wisdom: listeners wouldn't (or couldn't) pay attention to something so demanding. Where a radio show like *This American Life* (which perennially sits atop the "most popular" list and which supported *Serial*) might tell three to five stories around a single theme each week, *Serial* wanted to test if it was possible to do the opposite: to tell a single story spread out over twelve weeks.

One strength of *Serial* was Sarah Koening, the host and co-executive producer. She was an experienced and skilled journalist, having worked for *The New York Times,* ABC News, and as a producer on *This American Life*. But while her experience accounts for the quality of the show, it doesn't account for its unprecedented popularity. Koening hoped that the twelve episode run might generate 300,000 downloads, but by December of 2014, *Serial* had been downloaded over 78 million times.[1] It would also go on to win a 2014 Peabody Award.[2]

Could anyone have predicted *Serial*'s success? Well, if you knew where to look, there were hints that people were ready for a show like *Serial*. For example, millions of people already listened to storytelling-based radio shows like *The Moth Radio Hour*, *Snap Judgment*, *Story Corp* and the aforementioned *This American Life,* so storytelling was alive and well on the radio. But not only on the radio was storytelling going through a bit of a revival. It was happening all across popular culture.

For instance, television has been moving away from sitcoms, a form that has dominated the last thirty years, and toward long-arch narrative shows like *Lost, The Sopranos, The Wire, Mad Men, Battlestar Galactica, Breaking Bad,* and *Parenthood.*[3] On-demand services like Netflix, Amazon Prime, and Hulu, have given producers room to take risks with form and subject matter. Shows like *Orange is the New Black, Transparent,* or *Girls* might have been canceled on traditional channels, if they had even been given the green light. Current television programming is so good at creating intriguing and complex characters and inserting them into emotionally fraught situations that John Landgraf, the CEO of the FX channel claimed America is at "peak television" and is now facing

---

[1] Patrick Daniel, "The Secret to 'Serial': An Afternoon with Sarah Koening," *Huffington*

[2] "Serial (www.serialpodcast.org)," The Peabody Awards, accessed November 5, 2015,http://www.peabodyawards.com/award-profile/serial.

[3] Admittedly these shows have run along side reality-TV shows like *American Idol, Survivor*, and *Jersey Shore*.

the problem of shows that are merely *good* stealing audiences from shows that are *truly great*.[4]

Yet, even if you don't watch much television, if you follow sports, you'll find strong narrative framing. There have always been the conventional sports stories like, "David vs. Goliath," "The Comeback," and "The Second-String Stepping Up." But in 1979, a start-up cable channel called ESPN gave people the ability to know everything about a player's life both on and off the field. Now, because of the Internet, when college or professional athletes appear in front of live and television audiences—on stages of grass, wood, or ice—we often know as much about their personal lives as their previous performances.[5] The drama over rivalries, personal scandals, potential trades, and statistical predictions can make it hard to tell the difference between *Monday Night Football* and *Friday Night Lights.*

Video games were once seen as the antithesis to sports and were dismissed as childish and anti-social. They are now serious business: massively popular and incredibly profitable. But while there is a great diversity in the *kinds* of games, many are narratively driven.[6] Where a puzzle game like *Tetris* (popular in the late

---

[4] Linda Holmes, "Television 2015: Is There Really Too Much TV?," npr.org, August 16, 2015, accessed November 10, 2015, http://www.npr.org/sections/monkeysee/2015/08/16/432458841/television-2015-is-there-really-too-much-tv.

[5] "Pro wrestling is pure fiction, but it only exaggerates what we find in legitimate sports broadcasting, where an announcer—a skilled narrative shaper—tries to elevate a game to the level of high drama." Jonathan Gottschall, *The Storytelling Animal: How Stories Make Us Human* (Boston: Mariner Books, 2013), 13.

[6] Lucy O'Brien, "The Future of Video Game Storytelling," www.ign.com, January 12, 2014, accessed August 21, 2015,http://www.ign.com/articles/2014/01/13/the-future-of-video-game-storytelling.

'80s and early '90s) consisted merely of a series of falling blocks, now a similarly popular puzzle game, *Candy Crush* (released 2012), places each puzzle within a series of train stops through various candy-themed lands. Even massively popular first-person shooters like *Call of Duty* and *Halo,* or action-adventure games like *Assassin's Creed,* are woven into a narrative framework, spinning out their own mythologies, texts,[7] and movies.[8]

Not to forget traditional book publishing, which remains strong in spite of its struggles to respond to the rise of digital publishing.[9] While independent books stores are shutting down, self-publishing—including e-books, blogs, and interactive stories—has thrown open the gate to anyone with a good story to tell. And like video games, forms that were once viewed as lowbrow, childish, or hard to categorize (like the graphic novel), are setting records in popularity, sales, and critical attention.[10] And yet, there are still plenty of traditional books like *Harry Potter*, *The Girl with the Dragon Tattoo*, *The Hunger Games,* or Harper Lee's *Go Set a Watchman* that create cultural touch points across class, geography, and generation.

---

[7] *Wikipedia,* s.v. "List of Novels Based On Video Games," accessed August 21, 2015,https://en.wikipedia.org/wiki/List_of_novels_based_on_video_games.

[8] Wikipedia contributors, "List of films based on video games," *Wikipedia, The Free Encyclopedia,* https://en.wikipedia.org/w/index.php?title=List_of_films_based_on_video_games&oldid=689643307 (accessed November 10, 2015).

[9] Megan Gibson, "E-Books Go Out of Fashion as Book Sales Revive," *Time* (Jan. 9, 2015): 1, accessed May 24, 2015,http://time.com/3661173/book-sales-increase-ereaders-slump/.

[10] "Comics and Graphic Novel Sales Hit New 20-Year High in 2014," Comichron, June 30, 2015, accessed August 21, 2015, http://blog.comichron.com/2015/06/comics-and-graphic-novel-sales-hit-new.html.

Which still doesn't answer the question, "Could anyone have predicted the success of *Serial*?" And truthfully, the answer is less important than recognizing that *Serial* wouldn't have been successful if the audience hadn't been ready for it. Stories and storytelling have always been part of life, but they were often dismissed as merely entertaining, occasionally illustrative, but solidly childish—a thing to be left behind as we grow into adulthood. They are rarely taken seriously as a form of public discourse. But even a cursory survey reveals that storytelling is being taken seriously in conversations about education, science, marketing, politics, art, and psychology. People are recognizing that storytelling has rhetorical power, transformative impact, and is a fundamental part of the human experience.

And yet, too few Christians are participating in these conversations. Too few are embracing storytelling with passion and intellectual rigor. One of the goals of this work is to move the conversation about story from the margins toward the center. Another goal is to provide a basic vocabulary for those people who feel the value of stories but can't articulate why. Failure in either of these two areas risks widening the divide between Christians and the world they want to reach. Sadly, this is too often the case. The world speaks the language of storytelling and is labeled "postmodern," while Christians speak about moral absolutes and are labeled "out of touch." This is why Chapter One asks the question: "Why are some Christians hesitant to embrace storytelling?"

Chapter Two begins to develop a vision of good Christian storytelling. It pokes at the question "What is a good Christian writer?" It examines how successful Christian writers understand their work—both what they do and how they do it. This will require a two-pronged approach—one that goes both wide and narrow—and will begin to sketch the picture of what it means to be both a writer and a faithful follower of Jesus Christ.

In order to add definition to this sketch, Chapter Three takes the conclusions of Chapter Two and asks, "Is there a way to develop these characteristics?" Or said another way, "Is there a distinctly Christian writing *process*?" The bulk of this chapter connects 'best practices' of writing instruction with traditional Christian spiritual disciplines. For example, it is commonly believed that good writers must be well-read. Likewise, Christians are encouraged to read their Bible. Can these practices inform and support each other?

Chapter Four moves toward the final question of the project, "Why should the Church care about stories?" It will walk through the rhetorical, social, personal, and theological strengths of storytelling and land us at our goal: to convince Christians that stories are not only a legitimate, but often the preferable form for communicating about things of great importance, such as faith, salvation, grace, love, and God.

And yet, ending after Chapter Four would stop in the ironic spot of writing an *academic* paper advocating for the benefit of *stories*. After all, if stories can bear the weight of important themes like love, salvation, and the search for the divine, shouldn't a story also be able to communicate what it means to be a Christian writer and why stories are so important? Chapter Five is such a story—a work of fiction—that embodies several of the points from earlier chapters. It is my attempt to participate, as a faithful Christian, in the storytelling renaissance.

Chapter One:

Why Some Christians Aren't Embracing Storytelling

Stories are as old as time and all around us. They are part of the Bible and often used by Jesus to tell people about the Kingdom of God. They are simple and powerful. And in a moment we will see that some Christians and institutions do, in fact, see storytelling as an essential part of Christianity. Yet, fiction ranks third in sales at Christian bookstores nationally, behind Bibles and non-fiction, and is quickly losing ground to candles, tote bags, and lotion.[11] The fiction this billon-dollar-per-year industry does produce are often a *type* of storytelling that writer Ron Hansen explains this way, "There's a kind of fiction, that kind that, unfortunately, some Christian bookstores prefer, which is evangelization and testimony. This is how my life was saved, where I found Jesus as my Lord and Savior. But that's not how Jesus himself would have told the story."[12] Popular fiction titles in Christian publishing lean toward conspiracy theory, Amish romance, historical thriller, or post-apocalyptic survival tale.

There is a reason that some Christians living in the United States might prefer nonfiction to fiction, but to understand this reason, we need to place ourselves along a specific trajectory of time—one that starts slowly with the early

---

[11] Sarah Eekhoff Zylstra, "Religious Fiction Sales Nosedive, Non-Fiction Soars," *Christianity Today*, 4/10/2015, 1, accessed December 10, 2015, http://www.christianitytoday.com/gleanings/2015/april/religious-fiction-sales-nosedive-non-fiction-soars.html.

[12] Dale Brown, *Conversations with American Writers: the Doubt, the Faith, the In-Between* (Grand Rapids, MI: Wm. B. Eerdmans Publishing Co., 2008), 173

church, picks up momentum with the Protestant Reformation, gains speed with the American Revolution, and reaches full tilt around the turn of the century with the invention of the Internet. Be warned: not all stops on this journey are pleasant.

The early church did not have what could be considered an art scene. According to church historian Justo L. Gonzalez, early Christians were simple people who were filled with joy at being chosen and loved by Christ the Lord. But because most were poor, their lives "took place in the drab routine in which the poor in all societies must live."[13] Any art they produced was based around their worship and life together. This included illustrations of biblical stories, icons of Christ, or decorative catacombs.

However, after Constantine converted to Christianity and made it the state religion, Christianity began to take on some of the features common to "imperial protocol."[14] Church buildings became much more elaborate, marked by majestic basilicas and intricate mosaics. Ministers donned vestments that heightened their station. Worship services often began with a processional, including a choir and incense—which were customs borrowed from the imperial court, which themselves drew on Jewish temple practices. Still, the subject of art was unchanged; mosaics remained mostly biblical scenes or images of people from Christian tradition (or wealthy patrons of the church). The only change was that the setting became more opulent, the materials of better quality, and the art more ornate.

---

[13] Justo L. González, *The Early Church to the Dawn of the Reformation* (San Francisco: Harper & Row, 1984), 101.

[14] González, 125

For the next thousand years, the Church and the nobility were the only significant social structures that supported art, because they were the only ones that could afford to. Most people did not have time for leisure or recreation. They were too busy trying to survive. This situation does not mean that significant works of art were not created. Some of the greatest works of western art are based on Christian tradition and were commissioned by the church. Though there were many, just the two most recognizable artists illustrate this point. Michelangelo gave us *David,* the Sistine Chapel, *Pieta,* and *The Last Judgment.* DaVinci created *The Last Supper*, the *Annunciation*, and *The Virgin and Child with St. Anne.*

During this time, while works like Dante's *The Divine Comedy* were being written, there wasn't a literary tradition that could rival the visual arts. There was simply no means to mass-produce books. There were local, oral, storytelling traditions, and even traveling theater, but it wasn't until the Gutenberg Press that it was possible to have books as we know them: uniform, portable, and relatively cheap compared to the hand-drawn labor-intensive volumes that came before. Which does not mean they were so cheap that just anyone could print them. It was still only the Church, the aristocracy, and the growing merchant class who could afford to print tracts and pamphlets as well as knew how to read them. And while mass literacy was still a long way off, the printing press began a paradigmatic shift in storytelling—away from being primarily a corporate, theatrical event and toward being an individual, mobile, and timeless artifact that would eventually become the novel.

Around this same time, and aided by Gutenberg's movable type, the Protestant Reformation was shattering the Catholic Church. For the purposes of this work, the reasons for this division are less important than the fact that the Protestant Reformation spun out a number of subgroups within Christianity, including Baptists, Anabaptists, Lutherans, Calvinists, Anglicans and various other groups that bloomed and faded over the next two hundred years. Furthermore, the implications of the Reformation were as political as they were religious, and many of these groups found themselves persecuted by, or even at war with, dominant political powers. These groups yearned for a place where they could escape persecution, live free, and practice their faith without fear of being run through with a pike. They turned their eyes to America.

This is the basis of what America celebrates every Thanksgiving. The people we call "pilgrims" were really a Puritan group fleeing persecution in England. But they were not the only group to flee to the "New World." In fact, refugee communities popped up all along the east coast of what we now call the United States, but were at the time, colonies of Britain.[15] However, if there remained any allegiance to the Church of England or to their European homelands, it was broken by American independence.

By the time the dust settled on the Revolutionary War, religious communities throughout the eastern United States would be marked by a tension between a desire to isolate themselves in order to protect their group's independence and a wish to participate in the American experiment of freedom,

---

[15] Justo L. Gonzalez, *The Story of Christianity*, 2nd ed., vol. 2, *The Reformation to the Present Day* (Philadelphia, PA: HarperOne, 2010), 244.

progress, and representative government—in several cases this participation was so strong that a person's standing in the religious community determined whether one could vote, hold office, or testify in court.[16] It was a tension between *isolation* and *participation* that continues to mark social, political, and religious conversations in America to this day.

During this time there was still not a large Christian literary scene. Many of the immigrant communities, in rejecting the churches of Europe, also rejected lavish, ornate art and baroque architecture. There were those Lutheran and Anglican churches who followed their European forbears by embracing art of a certain piety, but many churches in the Reformed, Puritan, and Presbyterian tradition designed churches that were simple, white, and unadorned. Clothing was black, functional, and modest. People read the Bible, but often avoided dancing and were suspicious of the theater—which they viewed as inherently duplicitous. Christian art remained biblical, literal, and patriotic.

However, because religious freedom was woven into the fabric of the United States, as time went on the threat of religious persecution began to lessen. Christian groups flourished and began to integrate into society in ways that brought them both political and economic influence. They started schools and colleges, established newspapers, composed music, held conventions, formed publishing houses, and held public office. Ironically, as these Christians began to prosper, many of them began to use their influence to persecute others.

---

[16] "The religious influence, for example, was very strong in the governments of early new England, where, without necessarily intending to, Massachusetts and it's fellow Puritan colonies advanced because of democracy." Mark A. Noll, *A History of Christianity in the United States and Canada* (Grand Rapids, MI: Wm. B. Eerdmans Publishing Co., 1992), 40.

Part of the reason for this was that many Christians saw their flourishing as a sign of God's blessing—not only to them as individuals, but to America in general. This belief justified a theology called Manifest Destiny. This was the belief that God wanted America to spread from the east coast across the country to the west coast. And, if God wanted it, the thinking went, it was justified to kill and displace native people, go to war with Mexico, and kidnap and enslave people from Africa. After all, if God had handpicked America as his chosen people, who were we to let a little thing like the humanity of people with darker skin get in the way? This view continues to be part of our campaign rhetoric, foreign policy stances, and the basic tenant of conservative talk radio shows like *The Rush Limbaugh Show*.

Intolerances and indifferences arose among Christians because in order to maintain the belief in American exceptionalism, Christian society has had to ignore the stories and experiences that did not fit this narrative. This has included invalidating the stories of native peoples, slaves, Mexicans, child labor, women, LGBTQ people, African-Americans, Japanese-Americans, Arab-Americans, people in poverty, victims of rape, victims of domestic violence, victims of gun crime, victims of hate crimes, and prisoners—anyone whose narrative does not fit the arch of personal agency, individual responsibility, and hard work that automatically yields financial blessing. For hundreds of years, white, protestant men have been able to do this. They have controlled the money, votes, and means of communication. They've told the story they wanted to tell and ignored or attacked any outlier narratives. The tension between participation and isolation did not go away once Christians had power; instead, it transformed into a question of letting *others* participate in society or forcing them to remain isolated.[17]

But this single social narrative became increasingly more difficult to maintain. There was a steady knocking at the door of people who were crying out that, "Your America is not *my* America." Writers like Fredrick Douglas, W.E.B. DuBois, James Baldwin, Martin Luther King Jr., Malcolm X, Maya Angelou, Toni Morrison, Cornel West, and Ta-Nahesi Coates represent the tradition of writers who had tried to rewrite the American narrative to include the stories of people of color. Virginia Woolf, Betty Friedan, Alice Walker, and Gloria Steinem and others tried to expand the American narrative to include women's experiences, pain, and struggles. And while the stories of people of color and women have been the most visible, there are writers working to expand the American narrative to include the stories of Americans of various ethnicities, sexualities, and life circumstances.

However, these marginalized voices were a relative trickle in comparison to the class-five rapids roaring about how great and wonderful and blessed America was. In 1984 Ronald Regan accepted the Republican nomination for President with a speech that referred to America as "a shining city on a hill." This image is found in Matthew 5:14 but also references a Puritan sermon of 1630

---

[17] "I have not forgotten the day a student came to class and told me: 'We take your class. We learn to look at the world from a critical standpoint, one that considers race, sex, and class. And we can't enjoy life anymore.' Looking out over the class, across race, sexual preference, and ethnicity, I saw students nodding their heads. And I saw for the first time that there can be, and usually is, some degree of pain involved in giving up old ways of thinking and knowing and learning new approaches. I respect that pain. And I include recognition of it now when I teach, that is to say, I teach about shifting paradigms and talk about the discomfort it can cause." bell hooks, *Teaching to Transgress: Education as the Practice of Freedom* (New York: Routledge, 1994), 42-43.

capturing the common notion held by the people of New England that the newly founded city of Boston would be both literally and figuratively a beacon in the darkness. This thread of American exceptionalism is woven throughout the first 200 years of American history. It is more visible at some times than others, but it never disappears. Even as minority groups celebrated the American Dream from which they were being excluded, they continued to push to tell their stories of struggle and injustice. And in 2001, two things happened that started to speed up the unraveling of this narrative of American exceptionalism: the attacks of September 11 and the Internet reaching a critical mass of people.

The attacks of September 11, 2001 catalyzed a shift in the American public consciousness. Many Americans reacted by being suspicious of people who looked vaguely Arabic, accepted the suspension of some basic rights though the Patriot Act, and measured the patriotism of their politicians by whether they wore a flag pin in their lapel. However, others started to ask critical questions about what role American foreign policy had played in creating a situation where people were desperate enough to radicalize and die for their beliefs. There was a social conversation about the collateral damage of economic polices that put America's need for oil above the needs of any other country—and even of other countries' sovereignty.

It was also around this time that the Internet reached a critical mass of people. Facebook and iPhones were still a number of years away, but according to the US Census Bureau, 2001 was when over half of the homes in the United Stand had computers in them and 42% had access to the Internet.[18] While media corporations still had a stranglehold on information, an open-source revolution had begun. As more and more people began to get their news online, minority narratives began to find strength in numbers. People were able to respond to one another in something called a "comments section"—a thing that had once been restricted to the dinner table and an occasional "letter to the editor." Social media would soon widen this highway of interpersonal interaction, and not only about news, but about all aspects of life. Now, not only would people have direct access to information, but they would also have an easy and direct connection to the people making the news and to other readers. Reaching a mass audience was no longer limited to those who had control over a newspaper, magazine, radio, or television program.

Of course, the Internet did not immediately provide the necessary *agency* to affect change, either on a personal or societal level, but it did offer an unprecedented ability to share the story of people who fell outside the dominant narrative. Which means that, over the last fifteen years, the narrative that God has specially chosen America as a "city on a hill" has been publically deconstructed over issues of race, gender, economics, sexuality, religion, media representations of people groups, housing, gentrification, capitalism, food ethics, urban planning, church abuse cover-ups, political corruption, the role of various lobbies, gun control, prison over-crowding, dependence on oil, and access to health care and education—to name a few.

---

[18] Eric C. Newberger, "Home Computers and Internet Use in the United States: August 2000," *Current Populations Reports*, September 2001, 1, accessed December 10, 2015, http://www.census.gov/prod/2001pubs/p23-207.pdf.

Because the mainstream Christian narrative had been so woven into the American narrative, this deconstruction of American exceptionalism via the introduction of outlier narratives was seen as threatening. This pushed some Christian industries, institutions, and significant individuals to become further suspicious of storytelling and more ensconced in the language of tradition, dogma, creeds, and confessions—even as they risked deepening the disconnection between themselves and the culture they confess to want to reach. Christians resisted storytelling because they had so much to lose.

In a 2015 article in *The Atlantic*, Julie Beck wrote that American culture believes in, "American optimism—things will get better!—and American exceptionalism—I can make things better!—and it's in the water, in the air, and in our heads." She notes how much of the time this is a helpful attribute, but that, "The trouble comes when redemption isn't possible. The redemptive American tale is one of privilege, and for those who can't control their circumstances, and have little reason to believe things will get better, it can be an illogical and unattainable choice."[19]

This is the privilege of white American males (like myself): we've been telling a story, but we think we were describing reality. Since our story *was* the social narrative, we didn't have to understand systemic economic poverty, institutional racism, or the subtlety of gender identity. Now, white, American males are being presented with the stories of people they could not have

---

[19] Julie Beck, "Life's Stories," *The Atlantic*, Aug 10, 2015, 1, accessed August 17, 2015, http://www.theatlantic.com/health/archive/2015/08/life-stories-narrative-psychology-redemption-mental-health/400796/.

conceived of ever hearing about just twenty years ago. These stories are complex, specific, and tragic. And white, American males are coming to grips with the fact that their basic assumptions about the world are wrong. Instead of being divinely blessed and standing on the mountaintop, they've actually been standing on someone's neck.

This realization is evoking two primary responses among white Christians. Either they rush to accept responsibility in order to avoid dwelling in the wound, or they deny that they have anything to do with the troubles of marginalized people. Each response reinforces the narrative of the particular subculture from which it came (example: conservative/liberal). But this is the selective exposure of the privileged. Both postures deny the full story: the former by not fully listening and the later by denial. This is a double injustice because people pushed to the margins of society often lack money, political influence, or social support; all they have is their stories.

And yet, there are those Christians who have chosen participation over isolation. These are writers who have tried to look at life in all its brokenness. They are confessing Christians *and* writers at the highest levels of literature. Flannery O'Connor (*Wise Blood, Mystery and Manners),* Madeline L'Engle (*A Wrinkle in Time, Walking on Water: Reflections on Faith and Art*), Maya Angelou (*I Know Why the Caged Bird Sings*), John Updike (*Rabbit Run*), Joyce Carol Oates (*The Faith of a Writer: Life, Craft, and Art*), Fredrick Buechner (*Speak What We Feel, Not What We Ought to Say: Reflections on Literature and Faith*), and Toni Morrison (*Beloved*) are a sampling. There are also some social locations where conversations of faith and story are happening, including Calvin College's *Festival of Faith & Writing,* Seattle Pacific University's MFA degree and its associated IMAGE Journal, as well as The Collegeville Institute.

If Christians want to be able to interact with a dramatically changing world, isolation is no longer an option. Christians need to be willing to take the time to listen to the stories of people who do not look like, sound like, or believe like they do. Even if, historically, isolation served to protect a persecuted people, and even if it were still possible to maintain a single, dominant narrative, doing so would require violence—violence we have seen evidenced throughout American history. What is required is what Barbara Brown Taylor calls the language of "beholding." As a preacher and teacher she recognizes the role of understanding what *should* be happening,[20] but she wonders if we aren't too eager to rush away from seeing what is. She writes that, "I have no idea where I am going either as a writer or a preacher, but I mean to stay in the beholding business as long as I can, following the same good advice that God seems to use on me: *show, don't tell.*" We live in a world of stories. If we can't speak the language of story—if we are obsessed with telling rather that showing—then all that is left is tribalism, self-justification, and irrelevant orthodoxy.

---

[20] In the theological sub-field of Practical Theology, Richard R. Osmer outlines a four-fold task of theology. These tasks are descriptive-empirical, interpretive, normative, and pragmatic. These tasks correspond to the questions: What is happening? Why is it happening? What should be happening? How do we get there? Christians often spend all their time on the *normative task*, focusing on what should be happening without first really seeing what *is* happening.

Chapter Two:

What is a Good Christian Writer?

I love books on writing. I own fifty-seven books related to writing. There are how-to guides, idea prompts, and books that outline fifty ways to plot your novel. My shelves hold books about creativity, inspiration, or the "spirituality" of writing. These books offer many things. For example, they offer the technical instruction that I may not have gotten in school (or wasn't ready for at the time). They provide inspiration, writing prompts, and suggest solutions to troubling plot points. They also offer reassurance against the voices in my head telling me that I don't have anything worth putting down on the page.

But these books are also a trap. They approach writing as if it is a single, uniform thing. As if writing can be deconstructed, ground into powder, digested, and reconstituted within us—a kind of literary tincture. I fall into their trap because I want so badly for this to be true. I want to be able to pick up a book on writing and find the *one thing I've been doing wrong!* When in truth, books on writing are a lot like books on weight loss: they can be fun, inspiring, and helpful, but they can also provide the *feeling* that you've taken a step toward accomplishing your goal when you haven't. In this way, they scratch the creative itch without requiring the hard work of *actually writing.* This can be equally true of attending conferences, forming a writing group, or promoting your work on social media.

There are other problems with these books as well. They make assumptions about the hierarchical value of different kinds of writing (literary vs. academic vs. popular). They frequently ignore cultural or socio-economic differences that influence the amount of time or support available to an aspiring writer. They sometimes make assumptions about goals, intended audiences, access to markets, vocabulary, tone, use of technology, and personal preferences. They make these assumptions because most aspiring writers are just like me: they want a simple formula for writing success. In order to provide it, books on writing need to overlook the specific needs, cultural differences, or individual situation of the would-be writer. It's the equivalent of providing a student with a standardized test when what they need is an individualized education plan (IEP).

Which is not to say there is nothing to be learned by studying the writers we admire. If we want to know what it means to be a Christian writer, we would do well to consider the work of writers like C.S. Lewis, Flannery O'Connor, Madeline L'Engle, and Joyce Carol Oates. Their books on writing should be included in any canon of what it means to write as a Christian.

However, to *limit* ourselves to these writers neglects the work of other great Christian writers—writers like Maya Angelou and Toni Morrison—who would qualify for consideration on their faith or literary merit alone. Further, there are Christians whose faith is harder to weigh down with the anchor of orthodoxy—people like David James Duncan, Paulo Coelho, or John Updike. And what of Thomas Merton, who is respected among the orthodox, but held some unorthodox views? He is a great writer, but should he be included? Is he *Christian* enough?

This means that in my quest to understand what a Christian writer should look like, I had two problems: first, that writing is not a single, uniform thing. And second, that the Christian faith is not a single, uniform thing. Therefore, if I wanted to study Christian writers, I had a problem of editorial selection: who gets canonized? Since there is no predetermined group of people who are inarguably good Christian writers, any grouping would be editorial—biased toward the preferences of whoever selects the group. If I'm setting the group and I haven't read Toni Morrison, I may not include Toni Morrison.

It was this dilemma that pushed me, in the spring of 2014, to undertake a two-pronged approached to understanding what it looks like to be a good Christian writer. The first part was to read as much as I could from successful Christian writers who had written or spoken on the writing process. However, before I could do this, I had to accept the limits of my selection process and therefore the limits of my conclusions. Secretly, part of me hoped that maybe *I* would be the one to find the literary key to unlock the secret to writing success. However, I could not forget that the only way to make definitive conclusions would be by ignoring outlier voices.

Where the first prong went broad, the second prong went narrow. It was an ethnographic study of the habits, attitudes, beliefs and practices of good writers at Western Theological Seminary, in Holland, Michigan. I chose this school because, first of all, as a student in their Doctor of Ministry program, I had access to students and faculty. Second, I chose them because they were Christians who were already doing a lot of writing. And third, it was a good context because there were structures available to compensate for my biases in selection[21] and questioning.[22]

The reason I chose ethnography is because it was a methodology that did not seek to iron out all the wrinkles in order to present a conclusive statement. Rather, ethnography

> [I]s a form of social research used by sociologists, anthropologists, historians, and other scholars to study living human beings in their social and cultural contexts. Participant observation is the hallmark of this kind of social research. Ethnographers go to the places where people live, work, or pray in order to take in first hand the experience of group life and social interactions.[23]

Ethnography names and accepts both the limits and the biases of the research. It also explores one specific situation; if there are insights that apply to other situations, those are left to the people *in those situations*. It is a methodology more concerned with description than prescription, and tries to create what

---

[21] Participants were identified through the office of the Academic Dean, who selected current M.Div. students and faculty with at least three years of teaching experience. They were interviewed as individuals and the recordings generated by these interviews were transcribed. These transcripts were analyzed for common and particular themes. Participant responses were anonymous and each person was given an opportunity to read a draft of the work and offer feedback.

[22] A notable limit of the research, as it applies to the broader goals of my project, is that many of these people were not engaging in writing *stories*, at least not as a requirement for their study. Even if I would guess that some of them wish that they were.

[23] Mary Clark Moschella, *Ethnography as a Pastoral Practice: an Introduction* (Cleveland, OH: Pilgrim Press, The, 2008), 25.

Clifford Geertz in *Interpretation of Cultures* calls "thick description": a rich, interconnected, multi-faceted picture of life in context.[24]

Within ethnography I used Robert O. Brinkerhoff's success-case methodology.[25] This means the research went in-depth (qualitative) with a few, specially selected cases to create a "thick description"[26] (ethnography) and by focusing on the instances where a desired characteristic (good writing) is present (success-case) it could identify the common and particular practices. Essentially, I asked a bunch of good writers what they thought about writing. Then I compared their answers with the wider literature on faith and writing. My thinking was that if I could find a resonance between the two sets of data, I would gain a clearer picture of what it looked like to be both a Christian and a writer.

The results were six characteristics:

1) Writers are people.

2) They read well.

3) They care about the craft of writing.

4) They embrace the vulnerability inherent in writing.

5) They write with their whole selves.

6) They write pastorally.

---

[24] Clifford Geertz, *Interpretation of Cultures* (New York: BasicBooks, 1973).

[25] Robert O. Brinkerhoff, *The Success Case Method: Find Out Quickly What's Working and What's Not* (San Francisco, CA: Berrett-Koehler Publishers, 2003).

[26] "Believing, with Max Weber, that man is an animal suspended in webs of significance he himself has spun, I take culture to be those webs, and the analysis of it to be therefore not an experimental science in search of law but an interpretive one in search of meaning." Geertz, 5.

There was one characteristic that was present in the popular literature, but that was conspicuously missing from the research results.

7) That Christian writers write with a prophetic voice.

Writers are People

Somewhere in a café in Paris, sits The Writer. He is bent over his lineless journal, chain-smoking, and drinking wine, even though it's only early afternoon. People walk by and whisper to each other phrases like, "starving artist," "misunderstood genius," "commune with the muse." The Writer is everything you are not. The Writer pals around with David Foster Wallace—erudite, academic, and ahead of his time. The Writer told Jack Kerouac to write *On the Road* on a mythical single scroll. The Writer is as reclusive as J.D. Salinger or Harper Lee. He saw J.K. Rowling's outlines for Harry Potter on bar napkins. He can outdrink Hemingway. The Writer is as self-destructive as Edgar Allen Poe or Hunter S. Thompson. He can match wits with Mark Twain. He can see the injustices of society better than Tolstoy, Dostoevsky, or Solzhenitsyn. The Writer is a *real* writer, because he embodies the craft. He is almost a different species—a demi-god above mortals. He is a Titan with a typewriter.

The Writer is also a myth. The myth of The Writer is as destructive as it is prevalent. It turns writers into members of a country club of the damned. It stops regular people from writing because they do not feel qualified; they assume they lack a certain *je ne sais quoi* to be a writer. It is bad when a critic crushes a writer's dream, but it is tragic when a writer sabotages herself out of fear.[27] Too often, original work is crushed under the weight of the writer's own sense of inadequacy.

The truth is, writers are just people who write. They contain within their ranks not only various personal preferences, but, like all people, they are affected by sickness, the weather, the seasons, hunger, thirst, or lack of sleep. They are busy raising families, paying bills and worrying about how long it has been since they changed the oil in their car. They have church obligations, diets they can't keep, and stiff backs in the morning. They have favorite television shows, sports teams, restaurants, and vacation spots. They are just as distracted by cute puppy videos on YouTube as anyone else.

Therefore, good writers are not something *other*. They do not have special access to the muse. They are not exempt from the pains or struggles of life. Even those people at the highest level of literature are a combination of talent, hard work, and luck. There are as many ways to write as there are writers. Michael Chabon (*The Amazing Adventures of Kavalier and Clay, Telegraph Avenue)* begins writing at 10:30 pm to accommodate his children. E.B. White (*Charlotte's Web*) needed silence to write while Stephen King (*Carrie, The Shining*) edits to heavy-metal music. Ray Bradbury (*Fahrenheit 451*) wrote everyday while Sheri

---

[27] "Resistance to writing is natural, especially when it involves difficult feelings. Understand that resistance emanates from judgment-of others and of ourselves. All judgment, implicit or explicit and regardless of degree, halts the evolution of thought, feeling, and motion. It freezes growth in relationship and in creativity. When observed consciously, however, resistance becomes dynamic and can work *for* us. The moment we acknowledge our resistance, it becomes a motivating force and inevitably stimulates change." Laura Cerwinske, *Writing as a Healing Art: the Transforming Power of Self-Expression* (New York: Perigee Books, 1999), 20-21.

Reynolds (*The Rapture of Canaan*) needs to take lengthy breaks from her writing schedule. Gary Schmidt (*Ok For Now*) has won the Newberry Honor twice, but still teaches college students.

This diversity of life-styles, personal preferences, and basic humanity showed up repeatedly at Western Theological Seminary. For example, there were people who majored in English as undergraduates,[28] but others who focused on history, theater, music, international relations, or religion. Some people had been formally trained in composition, but others never held a passing interest in gerunds, participial phrases, or the correct use of a semi-colon.[29] Students and faculty alike had time constraints, life circumstances, and personalities that created limits to their writing, but each also found their own unique way to write in the midst of life's messiness.

Good Writers are Good Readers

A universal truth is a rare thing, but this comes close: all good writers read. They read widely—not restricting themselves to the genre in which they write or wish to write. They read not only fiction and nonfiction, but also the sub-genres within each category: poetry,[30] science fiction,[31] travelogues,[32] westerns,[33] fantasy,[34] young adult literature,[35] and memoir.

---

[28] Michael: "In college I was a double major, full major, in both philosophy and English"

[29] Gayle: "I've not taken a lot of grammar. I don't like grammar."

[30] Janet: "I read a lot of poetry I read a lot of things, I think reading in general has been the been best teacher I've had."

They also read *deeply*. For example, within a genre, good writers know that part of being a good reader is finding the right books.[36] This is not always as simple as ingesting the most popular books or reading the books on a course syllabus—a fact that became apparent to Michael, [37] a well-published professor, early in his career:

> One of the things I noticed in my first few years of teaching is that most books assigned in seminary are not written for seminary students. They are written for other scholars because that's what the guild gives incentive for. And it's students trying to *overhear* what scholars are saying to each other. That's not actually very helpful.

Assigning academic texts and expecting students to write for non-academic audiences is a bit like teaching cellular biology and expecting students to be prepared to work as a zookeeper. This is why good writers manage their reading. They aren't suspicious of their reading, but they recognize that a book

---

[31] Rose

[32] Franklin

[33] Robin

[34] Rose

[35] Penny: "When I was young I read a lot of children's books, obviously, which were fine but I also wound up in the less eloquent genres of children's writing quite often. Which would be mystery novels, dollar store checkout lane books."

[36] Stewart: "One of the big things is knowing the right books to read. Even doing the research to figure out what the important books are rather than people simply rehashing the same material one more time. To really find the right things is a bit of a challenge and then once you read those things you feel a lot more confident."

[37] All names have been changed.

can be rich in content but poor in form.[38] They recognize that a single book (or even several) has limits and therefore push themselves (and their professors) to find alternative voices or visions.

To this end, a couple of professors interviewed occasionally told students to learn from the text, but not to emulate an author's writing style.[39] When students were struggling to grasp a difficult concept, they may offer an alternative text that is more accessible. However, they did this hesitantly, recognizing that new understandings usually require struggle. They wanted to balance "spoon-feeding" students with abandoning them to drown in a difficult text. One professor, Stewart, tried to expose students to a range of readings, he said that, "I have kind of the basic stuff. [Students] may not consider it basic, but things that are easier. Then I have what I consider "stretch" material. I want to stretch people a little bit, as well as give them things they can read and feel good about because they understand."

Not only do good writers read, but they also know how to use what they read.[40] While a lot of reading stems from curiosity—as opposed to looking for support for a pre-formulated argument—good writers are able to balance their

---

[38] Penny: "Read really good things and pay attention to the way they structure their sentences, the way that their arguments flow. Pay attention to the way that they use of verbs."

[39] Stewart: "I assigned a lot of writing that told people, "I don't think this is very good writing. So don't emulate it. But here's the content you should be getting out of it." So I think I tend to, when push comes to shove, I'll go for content over just the beauty of the writing."

[40] Gayle: "I realized starting that way I began looking for sources that fit into my what I *wanted* the paper to stay. I was trying to fit into, you know, so it was kind of roadblock. But once I realized I need to stop looking for sources that say what I want them to say, it's sort of help me balance my opinion with other sources and start plugging in quotes and then really just general ideas from different authors and how they connected together. It was just a really good way to begin kind of small and start expanding rather than just go here's a paper. Which I've done."

own words with the words of others. Some good readers give their curiosity a long leash, even incorporating their wider, non-academic reading into their academic work.[41] Bonnie, a student who was, in her own words, "a big fan of fiction," always tried to find a narrative element to weave through her academic work.[42] Some readers of poetry hoped their prose would have a lyric beauty. Tanya, a student close to graduation, explained her desire that, "even in academic papers, to have it not sound really stuffy and dry, but to have those papers have life and vibrancy. To feel engaging and like I paid attention to the words that I was using."

Still, there were writers who kept their academic writing separate from their personal writing. They did this either because they were more comfortable within the parameters of academic writing or because they don't feel confident to incorporate a story without being moralistic or to use a poetic element without being sentimental. Robin, a professor who cares deeply about writing, admitted that, "I'm not so good at bringing in the stories, the human interest hook. That's why I feel more at home in the academic setting where you don't really need that hook. The hook is the thinker. And the person has to read it because it's in their field."

That good writers are good readers is so prevalent among the wider literature it could almost be taken as gospel. Susan Sontag (*In America*)

---

[41] Penny: "I tell stories. I will think about a scripture passage and see the pattern or the rhythm and find a similar rhythm or a similar pattern in life here and now."

[42] One of the things that helps me with paper writing is that I almost always start with a story. I don't care if it's church history [or] if it's theology. It is very unusual for me not to have a story that I've made up or from my personal life. I like having that story, whether it's a paragraph or a page, then draw the requirement for the paper through that story.

summarized this fact: "Reading, the love of reading, is what makes you dream of becoming a writer. And long after you've become a writer, reading books others write—and rereading the beloved books of the past—constitutes an irresistible distraction from writing. Distraction. Consolation. Torment. And, yes, inspiration."

Anne Lamott (*Traveling Mercies, Hard Laughter*) represents many writers who found comfort in books starting at a young age.

> I read more than other kids; I luxuriated in books. Books were my refuge. I sat in corners with my little finger hooked over my bottom lip, reading, in a trance, lost in the places and times to which books took me. And there was a moment during my junior year in high school when I began to believe that I could do what other writers were doing. I came to believe that I might be able to put pencil in my hand and make something magical happen.

Nevertheless, however much she wanted to "make something magic happen," Anne Lamott still needed to do the hard work of writing. She still needed to work on her craft.

Good Writers are Craft Writers

Everyone can write, but not everyone can write well. Even for the most talented, good writing is really hard work. For experienced writers there are no synonyms. They can debate the differences between *begin, ensue,* and *start.* They stress over semi-colons. They study the tradition, the current trends, and the creative process. This is not something they do only on the weekends (though some may only have the weekends available to do it). There is a level of seriousness and professionalism to their work. Madeline L'Engle writes about honing her craft that,

> [We must] let go whatever we may consider our qualifications. There's a paradox here, and a trap for the lazy. I do not need to be "qualified" to play a Bach fugue on the piano (and playing a Bach fugue is for me an exercise in wholeness). But I cannot play that Bach fugue at all if I do not play the piano daily, if I do not practice my finger exercises. There are equivalents of finger exercises in the writing of books, the painting of portraits, the composing of a song. We do not need to be qualified; the gift is free; and yet we have to pay for it.[43]

Each writer interviewed admitted they have to "pay" for their writing. For example, Tanya admitted, "I think I pay attention to how it looks, how it sounds—instead of just dashing something off." There were several points where writers took care with their work: in identifying the audience, selecting the right genre, and in polishing the details of grammar and punctuation.

It was a common sentiment among the students interviewed that they questioned *for whom* they were writing when they wrote academic papers. But even as a professor, Robin admitted that one of her biggest struggles as a writer was the struggle to understand her audience. Likewise, Michael noted how changing the supposed audience changes the elements of a piece, saying that, "a paper is not a paper is not a paper." Meaning, that to write something for "the NPR crowd"[44] is different than writing for blog readers, which is different than

---

[43] Madeleine L'Engle, *Walking On Water: Reflections On Faith and Art* (Colorado Springs, CO: WaterBrook Press, 2001), 76.

[44] Stewart: "I remember Ellen Cherry once said she's writing for the NPR audience. And so there's a certain level of education I think I would anticipate and those are the people that I think I write to."

writing for a professor.[45] A writer's intended audience will dictate the length, vocabulary, tone, use of the 1st person, citation requirements, assumptions, and the scope of the piece. When the audience is unclear it is hard to move forward in the writing process. Most often, when a good writer stalls in their writing or when their writing doesn't resonate, it is likely they are unclear about the intended audience for their work.

If the audience *is* clear, good writers know the strengths and limits of each genre and are able to work within them.[46] In an academic context, most of the students were able to write a solid academic paper.[47] But several noted how, when there was flexibility in permissible forms, they took full advantage to push the limits.[48] While they recognized the importance of pairing the right form with the right audience, they also saw how digital media is making it easier to integrate photos and videos, solicit reader response through social media, and produce high-quality material at a low cost (and with little oversight). Michael saw a potential pitfall for a seminary that continues to focus entirely on traditional academic writing. Saying that,

---

[45] Franklin: "I write my papers to be read by professor. So I'm writing with what I think they'll want to hear in mind."

[46] Michael: "There isn't such a thing as a neutral genre, like you can do certain things with blogs and you can't do certain things. Certain things don't work well with blogs. You can do certain things with Facebook, and certain things do *not* work well with Facebook."

[47] Franklin: "Back to basics. I think I lost a lot in college of just basic, thesis, argument, have good quotes, find the right quotes. I think I lost a lot of that and I think coming back to seminary, it sounded so silly, I think someone said it in one of my Junior level classes, "We're not looking for anything fancy. You don't need to 'wow' us with your *magnum opus*, just write a thesis and get your arguments down." And I was like, "That's so boring." But I think that's actually *still* some of the hardest papers I have to write when professors ask that of me."

[48] Penny: "All she said was at the end of the semester, you're going to turn in some sort of final project. It can be a book review. It can be a research paper. It can be an adult education class. It can be pretty much anything you want it to be as long as related to this class and some significant question."

I would like to see more graduates entering into writing of various sorts in their pastoral ministry. I do feel there needs to be more critical, theological reflection through some of the issues of genre and some of the traps that pastors can fall into. Social media has built-in genre limitations and I think people tend to think of it just as "words" or "digital information" and it's not. They're genres. And I think there is a place for it, but it's pretty hazardous too. I think pastors can really make mistakes if they don't understand what is inherent in these genres.

Some research participants struggled to understand their audience. Some had difficulty with particular genres of writing. But none were particularly worried about proper grammar, accurate punctuation, or proper citation. They simply assumed that these things were part of the craft of writing. Bonnie summed up the common sentiment by saying, "It is only after you have mastered those rules that you're allowed to take liberties...You have to master the rules, otherwise they master you." Still, several students noted how the faculty's fanaticism for accurate citation caused an unproductive anxiety among the student-body. Franklin said that,

We spend so much time fighting about what footnotes to use. And what kind of citation. And there's anxiety about *formatting* but that's about the only thing. There's a regular sort of reminder, 'This is the kind of citation to use. This is the kind footnote to use.' I think students feel anxiety to make sure that their formatting is correct. I think, for whatever reason professors have given marks out, against bad formatting but then not so much about the actual content.

Still, even if they feel anxiety, good writers have a plan for how they are going to write. There are various methods for getting the job done, but most writers were aware of their own particular process. They recognized the limits of time, the relative importance of the piece, and the amount of energy they had available. Time management is critical to writing well. And yet, this was a struggle for both students and professors. A common reason writers in this context didn't get feedback on their work, do multiple drafts, or avoid easily correctable mistakes is because they hadn't budgeted enough time. Robin wished she got more feedback on her work, but admitted that, "part of [not getting feedback] is I'm not naturally inclined to do that, but another part is time. I'm usually scrambling to meet a deadline." Any number of research participants could have said the exact same thing.

Good Writers Embrace Vulnerability

When I asked her about her writing process, Robin laughed and said, "The word 'anguish' comes to mind." She was not alone in this sentiment. Many comments swirled around the emotional weight of writing. And while not everyone used the same language, most of it boiled down to an understanding that good writing requires some level of vulnerability.

First off, there is the vulnerability of the blank page. Tanya explained it this way: "there's something intimidating when there are no words on the page and there's plenty of other tasks in life to do. It feels like, "Oh no! There's this big thing I have to approach again." It takes courage to step out onto the blank page, because you are accompanied by the fear that, this time, the words won't come. There's that whisper in your ear that anything good you've written in the past was a fluke and everyone will finally see you for the fraud you are. This state of fear is as true for the first year seminary student as it is for the successful writer.[49]

But there is a second type of vulnerability that occurs: the vulnerability of sharing your work with other people. Penny summed it up well when she said, "It's one thing to write for yourself, where you sort of know your own language, but its another thing to have someone else read your writing and say, 'What does this mean?'" Likewise, Rose spoke about how, "If they're critiquing my writing, they're critiquing me. Sometimes I wonder am I going to be strong enough to take it if someone says, 'This is terrible! Your writing's horrible! This doesn't work!' There's always some anxiety. There's always some."

Sharing your writing opens you to critique—both of style and content, but it also opens you to approval and praise, which can sometimes prove harder to accept. In fact, when participants were told that they were included in the research because they were identified as good writers, many reacted with surprise,[50] disagreement,[51] or qualification.[52]

---

[49] Fredrick Buechner "What robs me of real gratification is what I think I inherit from my past, the feeling of "if they only knew." W. Dale Brown, *Of Faith and Fiction: Twelve American Writers Talk about Their Vision and Work* (Grand Rapids: William B. Eerdmans Publishing Co., 1997).

[50] Janet said how, "I never really identified with being a writer, that was never something I saw myself as, because I always had friends who were really good writers. *They* were the writers. *They* were the ones who have college degrees. *They* were the one who really good. So I never really saw myself that way."

[51] Gayle said "I think I have a lot of ideals about writing, about an idea of what a good writer looks like and I don't think I'm in it. I don't think I'm it."

[52] Franklin: "And I'm not sure if I get to be considered a writer. I write, but not as a lifestyle or as a rhythmic thing but as a kind of, as an assignment, or as a requirement. I know I'm expected to write for this institution and I try to write well, but I'm surprised someone considered or pointed to me as a good writer. Specifically because I think that I have a lack of discipline, or I don't think I have the qualities of someone who spends time and energy and regular space writing.

The necessity of vulnerability in writing is inarguable, but there are three different responses to this fact: paralysis, perfection, and feedback. *Paralysis* happens when a writer is so overwhelmed by the blank page that they can't even begin. All they can see is the potential futility of their effort, the enormity of the task, or the raw nerve they aren't strong enough to expose. They simply *can't* write.[53] Even those writers who have learned to deal with writing paralysis still wrestle with blocks from time to time. One example would be Franklin, who had stopped writing anything beyond that which was required for class. He felt confident in his abilities, but he also spoke about the anxiety of sharing his writing:

> Am I performing at a level appropriate? Am I growing? Am I improving? Am I writing at a level that [the faculty] think I should be writing at? That sort of productive anxiety. On my blog some of that anxiety gets pretty selfish and petty. Do people like me? Are people going to like this post? If someone stumbled upon this blog and read this article will they become a follower? Will they share this with others? I think that's some of the reason why I haven't been [writing] as regularly.

The second way that writers deal with vulnerability is by striving for *perfection*. They try to conquer the blank page by sheer force of will. Typically, this group has done well in school, getting good grades by writing to the

---

I've been told I put thoughts on a page well, that I have good grammar and can put things in mechanically correct ways. I don't feel like I've earned the right to call myself a writer."

[53] Robin spoke about doubt that accompanies her, "I would rather people I *don't* know read my writing than people I *do* know. There's something about people I know that I probably care more about what they think. I have to really push myself to share my writing. And there have been many times when I have been up late in the night writing something that feels fairly obscure thinking, "Really? Is this worth it?"

expectations of their teachers.[54] They might write a single draft of high-quality prose, but frequently will wait until the deadline to do so. By waiting until the last minute, they minimize the time for revision. For the perfectionist, it is better to have it done and out of her hands than have to accept that they might have been able to do better. [55] Robin is a self-identified perfectionist, "Most of the time, I have done very little revision. Usually I write, I get maybe a few feedbacks—because I'm detail oriented, I don't have a lot of typos—I hardly ever do revision."

Now, perfectionism can come from a place of fear, but for someone like Robin, it can also come from a desire to do justice to the subject she's writing about. She explained how "there's a whole layer of anxiety around wanting to be faithful and accurate, not in just a legalistic way, but faithful to what God has revealed and feeling the weight of trying to represent really big doctrines." And, as noted before, time management is always a concern for writers, so being able to handle a certain amount of work without needing extensive feedback can save time and energy. While all writing is improved by getting feedback, the reality is that there is not always time in a busy schedule to get extensive feedback. Of course, knowing *when* to handle something on your own and when to seek help is a skill all its own.

---

[54] Tanya: "I was always a good student growing up in grade school and did not like to bring attention to that, I needed to fit in. I didn't want to be weird. To brag about my writing feels weird."

[55] Gayle: "I think that the graduate level its scary to me. I don't know, I'm an adult now come on...I don't know. I would assume that academic expectations are a lot higher and I don't want my paper to get torn apart before I handed in. Even if it gets torn apart after I hand in."

And yet, making time for *feedback* is the third way good writers deal with the vulnerability of writing. In this way, they move toward the vulnerability and make it helpful and productive. Yet, good writers do not share their work with whoever is willing to read it. Instead, they manage their feedback process[56] by being deliberate about what kind of feedback they want,[57] who they trust to read their work,[58] and when in the process they're ready to share their writing.[59]

Interestingly, many of the students in this research used *faculty* critique as the primary (often only) form of feedback,[60] deferring to the faculty because of their expertise. Plus, the students believed that most of the faculty genuinely wanted them to succeed,[61] even if, as Susan said, "it's easy to get defensive when you don't get a good grade on something." Unfortunately, most of the feedback

---

[56] Gayle: "I don't really enjoy group peer editing. It's a little intimidating to me just a lot of opinions and, I don't know. I've had experience with that with paper not paper even, just the essay just sort of gets torn apart gingerly, nicely, kindly, but by a lot of people. Everybody's opinion adds up to one like, 'Man that sucked.' And I just don't really enjoy that very much."

[57] Michael: "But if I want pastors and students to be reading something I almost always have reading groups work with me with drafts... [They are pulled] from the audience, so I'll often pull together students maybe have a pizza lunch or something on an article. And for all of my books, I've had reading groups with people from the audience. Especially with students, pastors, and scholars."

[58] Rose: "[It] can be really difficult to say, 'Okay I'm going to let you read this. I'm going to let you critique this.' I'm not good at being vulnerable. I'm not good at the opening myself up. I think that's one of the reasons I like writing=because its one of the ways I'm *able* to be vulnerable."

[59] Janet: "I don't show my stuff to people on till I'm ready to shown. So for good or for evil, what I call final draft nobody gets to see it until I call it a final draft."

[60] Gayle: "I think if I gave myself more opportunity to capitalize on feedback and actually use it I might enjoy it more. I don't because I think I kind of live paper to paper academically. It just kind of sits there as a critique. I just wonder if I could use it as more of a constructive tool.

[61] Robin: "And I am one who definitely looked at the feedback I got as a student and tried to incorporate that."

came too late, in the form of comments on a graded assignment rather than integrated into various aspects of the writing process—like brainstorming, outlining, research, drafting—where feedback might make a more significant difference on the final product.

This touches on one of the problems of trying to write well in an academic context: grading. Assigning a grade is a very definitive evaluation of a writer, one that reinforces a power dynamic which may actually work against vulnerability.[62] If the only feedback comes from a professor, and then only at the end of the semester (through the simplistic form of a letter-grade), rather than through a semester-long participatory feedback process, then students will either be forced to develop systems of feedback outside the classroom or to write in a guarded way, adapting their style and content to the specific proclivities of each professor. Building faculty feedback into a course isn't always fun or easy, for either the faculty or the student, but when done well, it can build long-term writing skills and confidence.[63]

There were two research participants who seemed more willing to embrace vulnerability than most. The first participant, Stewart, showed very little anxiety about sharing his work. He explained that he saw writing less as a quest for perfection than a necessary exchange on the road to understanding. He said,

---

[62] Is traditional grading, however motivational it may be, at cross-purposes to developing good writers? Does is prevent people from seeing writing (and perhaps all learning) as an act of worship? In this context, the seminary also grants denominational students their *Certificate of Fitness for Ministry* which is required for ordination. This added evaluation may exacerbate student apprehension to say or write anything that jeopardizes their personal interests. How can the seminary become a safe environment for the vulnerability of writing while at the same time making evaluations of student's academic and personal merit?

[63] Michael: "I think it adds confidence as I bring it to a broader audience."

I feel quite good about [feedback], but I also don't see it as having to have had achieved perfection. I'm interested to see how other people will interact with it. Whether or not it resonates with them. Certainly if they find errors, I'm interested in that. But also different ways that people might see things, which is always surprising to me, how everyone is looking at the world from very different lenses. It's always intriguing.

The other person was Jesse, a student who saw his writing as *worship*. He said that, "I write in a personal way. I prepare myself to open up to people and not be afraid. When I view [writing] as a gift from God—that God would be with me when I share pieces of myself—then [I've been], not rewarded, but definitely blessed in my vulnerability."

It isn't just writers in this project who have some level of fear and insecurity about their writing. Writers everywhere carry pockets of vulnerability, fear, and insecurity about their work. Garrison Keillor writes that, "[Writing] can be pleasurable, but only if the material you write is good. If it's not, you're filled with self-loathing. If the material is good and funny, you still loathe yourself, of course."[64] Reflecting on her life as a writer, Susan Sontag wrote, "What you accumulate as a writer are mostly uncertainties and anxieties."[65] And John Steinbeck wrote that,

> I suffer as always from the fear of putting down the first line. It is amazing the terrors, the magics, the prayers, the straitening shyness that assail one. It is as though the words were not only indelible but

---

[64] George Plimpton, "Garrison Keillor, the Art of Humor No. 2," *The Paris Review*, Fall 1995, 1, accessed November 28, 2015, http://www.theparisreview.org/interviews/1551/the-art-of-humor-no-2-garrison-keillor.

[65] Susan Sontag, "Directions: Write, Read, Rewrite. Repeat Steps 2 and 3 as Needed.," *New York Times*, December 18, 2000, accessed July 16, 2015, http://www.nytimes.com/2000/12/18/arts/18SONT.html?pagewanted=1.

that they spread out like dye in water and color everything around them[66]

But perhaps Anne Lamott paints the best picture of the vulnerability of writing:

> [T]he bad news is that if you're at all like me, you'll probably read over what you've written and spend the rest of the day obsessing, and praying that you do not die before you can completely rewrite or destroy what you have written, lest the eagerly waiting world learn how bad your first drafts are.[67]

Good Writers are Integrated Writers

Writing can feel like an insurmountable task. How then, do good writers do it? How do they find time to not only to pay their bills, raise families, maintain friendships, but also read books, work on the craft of writing, and pour out their heart? The answer is that they are *personally integrated.*

They do not see themselves as *sometimes* a writer, as if writing were a mask they could remove when it is inconvenient. They are a writer from dawn to dusk and in their dreams. Writing is not a box to be checked, but an expression of themselves, in some cases an *artistic* expression. The artistic element is significant because good writers know there is a difference between getting an "A" on a paper and being a good writer. Proper punctuation can get good

---

[66] John Steinbeck, "The Art of Fiction No. 45 (Continued)," *The Paris Review*, Fall 1975, 1, accessed July 16, 2015,http://www.theparisreview.org/interviews/4156/the-art-of-fiction-no-45-continued-john-steinbeck.

[67] Anne Lamott, *Bird by Bird: Some Instructions On Writing and Life* (New York: Anchor, 1995), 8.

grades.[68] Writing toward the grading rubric can get good grades.[69] A modest

investment in craft can get good grades.[70] But integrated writers believe that

writing is important, not just for school, but because it is an expression of life and

faith.[71] Alice captured what many integrated writers feel when she said,

> I learn about the world through writing. I might experience things
> in the world, but when I write, I sit down and I think about those
> things, what I've learned or what I felt, and through that I learn
> about what's going on or about my interaction within the world.

Most writers are deeply curious about the world. They use writing to help

focus their attention on the world around them and make sense of their

experiences. They are open to being surprised by what they discover, even when

what they discover isn't pleasant.[72] Therefore, writing is part of a larger posture of

engagement[73] that may also include teaching,[74] lecturing, running a workshop,

---

[68] Tanya: "I didn't think I worked that hard on, and I got it back with an "A." And the professor said, you'd be amazed at how helpful it is to just put commas in your sentences. Like, 'Use correct grammar and I will give you an A.'"

[69] Gayle: "Every professor is different, some literally want you to hit point ABCD and then be done. Here's some point ideas for point A. Here's some ideas for point B. But regardless it's hard for me to make sure that I'm fitting within kind of a not really a box, I don't want to be unfair, because of the useful box."

[70] Rose: "Well I think that the first thing is to *care*. I think, uh, there's a lot of things I like about Western one of the things I don't think they do well is to encourage good, to insist on good writing I guess. And so I think that invites people not to care about their writing. So yeah, I would want to tell a student to be invested in."

[71] Robin: "I'm thinking that imagination and the beauty is really important as part of our faith"

[72] Penny: "When I encounter a really difficult situation or when I encounter something that I don't understand, then I'll sit down and I can *think* about it for days. But until I write it out there will be no resolution to any of it. That's sort of the writing as catharsis. But at the same time writing is also, because writing is how I process the world, it doesn't always end where I wanted to. So its kind of right like sermon writing in that you think is going to a particular direction and you get to the end of it and you're like, "I really didn't want to hear that.""

reading, or talking to friends and colleagues.[75] Yet, there remains something special about writing that solidifies an ephemeral idea in a way these other methods do not. Rose spoke of how, "I think [it's] a continuing effort to know who I am, to have an honest engagement with myself, because I think if I'm not doing that [then] my writing isn't as good." And Alice captured the interplay between good writing and self-knowledge,

> If I'm engaging with myself, my writing overall will be better. My writing is going to be more honest, more aware. My writing isn't as shallow. If I'm feeling something and I'm trying to push it to the side or ignore it, it's [still] there, popping up. And that can hurt my writing.

Living integrated lives allows writers in a hectic academic context to look for ways to integrate their learning. Several people leveraged connections between their classes in order to save time.[76] Some developed a meta-theme over a semester's work to be able to draw on the same research. Still others mentioned slanting an assignment toward their interests,[77] even adapting an assignment's

---

[73] Penny: "I think the ability to speak truthfully about things is one of my favorite qualities in writers, because writing is how I process things. And so it hasn't really happened until I written about it."

[74] Michael: "There are certain times in class where I have a kind of "Ah, ha!" moment by the way a student question is raise or something like that. So sometimes it happens verbally. But it's not really made as concrete until its written."

[75] Stewart: "I've been thinking about this for 5 years. So I've been reading and working and doing all that too. I'm also working on an article... And things build, [it's] hard to say because rarely do you start fresh on a whole subject matter. I mean, you're building on years of experience."

[76] Gayle: "So I was trying to figure out how I could obviously maintain academic integrity but still do well in this overwhelming environment, sort of still have focuses. What I've kind of developed is the system of choosing one or two things that really kind of, well almost form like this meta-narrative over all my classes."
[77] Michael: "The class was largely about 5th century Christologies and I was able to make connection points and explore it for myself."

format when necessary.[78] This was not done entirely as a matter of efficiency but because integrated writers are engaged with the world in a way that touches their hearts.

Just as integrated writers write *from* the heart, they also write *to* the heart.[79] They try to connect with readers in a way that touches the mind and moves the heart. In this way, integrated writers assume an integrated reader. Stewart said that,

> I think people are more driven by their desires than their minds. And their minds are usually used to backup their desires. So I think changing people's desires is just as important...So I think a lot about beauty and what beauty does in order to lead people into the next step, in whatever [I'm] doing through writing.

This style of writing—from the heart, to the heart—yields writing that is full of the writer's voice. A writer's voice is her style, the unique character that runs across her work. It may be a sense of wonder,[80] detailed precision,[81] or a sense of humor that is snarky[82] even boarding on inappropriate.[83] For Janet,

---

[78] Penny "And I'm not going to pull out, 5 years from now, a theology of leadership paper and sit there and read through everything I should be doing. But what I *might* do is go back to these six letters to my future self with these things that I want to remember. And a little bit of advice for myself. It definitely made it more emotionally involved."

[79] Janet: "And so relying heavily on stories to tell messages instead of just facts."

[80] Tanya: "I'm not sure it comes across this way, but sort of a wonder at the world and its beauty and then kind of consoling myself that I don't always, um, make space to take it in."

[81] Robin: "My writing, you could *possibly* say its beautiful for academic writing. It's clear. I'm a good translator. I can take ideas that are complicated and try to make them accessible, try to write fairly clearly."

[82] Gayle: "I tend to get a little snarky in my writing. I like comedy. I love satire. So if I can bring that in at all its my favorite. So satire and comedy I think speak a lot of truth in small portions."

giving her voice room to play was what gave her the courage to participate in a rigorous academic setting. She said,

> I'm not going to be the best systematic theology thinker out there. I'm not going to be the best at remembering dates and events in history. But what I can do is take the things I have learned from those classes and give my voice to them. [I can] make them somewhat relevant for today.

This too, is in keeping with the wider literature of writers reflecting on writing. Silas House (*A Parchment of Leaves*) says that, "People always think that writers are smarter than other people. That's the biggest hoax in the world. I just think writers are the ones who are looking in different ways; they're observing what a lot of other people take for granted, and just writing it down." If we're going to write well, it is going to take all we have to offer.

Good Writers are Pastoral Writers

In the seminary interviews, there was an understanding of writing that was not found in the wider survey, at least not with the same language: that good writers try to be *pastoral* writers. A pastoral writer tries to write in the same spirit of hospitality they would display when hosting a guest in their home or meeting someone for the first time. In the seminary context, many of the parallels people

---

[83] Janet: "I'm not the kind of person who, if something is silly or, you know, random…even if its bordering on inappropriate I'll usually air on the side of being inappropriate, not for inappropriateness sake, but just because I think its funny

drew related to the church: the hospitality required when speaking from the pulpit, when serving the bread and the wine, or when baptizing a new believer.[84]

Pastoral writers believe that writing can be a calling. They understand it to be God's will that they write. This belief could easily result in an attitude of arrogance, but more often people spoke against writing for self-promotion[85] or writing to show how well they used words or how superior a writer they were.[86] Instead, a pastoral writer writes to build a more expansive vision of the Kingdom of God. They may write critically, but with tenderness. Michael explained this,

> I do not want to write with bitterness or anger or in any sort of self-protective mode. Let's be creative and gracious and assume the best of our readers—try to open up a more expansive vision of what God is doing. If I have to criticize people on the way, I will do it, but I'll try to do it graciously. And it's that positive constructive task which has got to drive it. I refuse to deconstruct without reconstructing, without giving an alternative vision that takes seriously the ministry concerns and tries to make a case for a more expansive positive vision.

This attitude of graciousness extends from subject to audience.[87] Stewart explains how respect for his audience influences the way he writes, "I want

---

[84] Franklin: "I hope when people read what I write they sense and can hear in the writing, a level of care, both for the words themselves and for the discipline of writing, but also for the reader. In that way I want to be a pastoral writer. Not just a pastor who writes but someone who writes pastorally. Someone who can communicate care and love and maybe even challenge and a certain transformational call within the writing."

[85] Franklin: "I think there's a kind of writing for a writer's voice that writes for self-promotion...And I think you can tell that if you're reading carefully."

[86] Franklin: "I think you read it in some news articles or in some blogs, you hear it in sermons sometimes, the writer or the speaker is using their words to show you how well, either how well their words are, or how well they use words, but mostly how great they are the writer or speaker. And I think you can tell that if you're reading carefully."

[87] Franklin: "I hope when people read what I write they sense and can hear in the writing, a level of care, both for the words themselves and for the discipline of writing, but also for the reader. In that way I want to be a pastoral writer. Not just a pastor who writes but someone who

people to know that I care. I care for my subject matter as well as my audience. And that I love what I'm doing…I think even a kind of gentleness with my intended audience. I want that to come out because, well, I'm a Christian." In this way, pastoral writers approach their writing from a sacramental posture. They don't attempt to master or control a subject by their knowledge or their writing acumen,[88] but rather honor and revere the deep theological and personal complexities of life.[89]

Interestingly, Michael noted how trying to write more pastorally can actually make you a more pastoral person. He explained that,

> There are different skills that will be developed through writing and these actually do relate to pastoral ministry. You can see it at any church council meeting or any general assembly, people who can't actually hear a perspective—other than their own—and express it in cogent terms. And certainly with theology it's a huge skill as well. It's a skill to find your own voice, but also to authentically hear the voices of others. And writing is a tool to help develop that skill.

Therefore, the good Christian writer will see what they do as a gift from God, but a gift meant for the good of other people. You don't need to be a pastor to write pastorally, but when you do, it can become an act of worship.[90] Out of

---

writes pastorally. Someone who can communicate care and love and maybe even challenge and a certain transformational call within the writing."

[88] Stewart: "there's a certain kind of writing where you want to lay out *every single detail* how to make sure that your reader knows you have total command of everything. I think that was part of what I wanted to do during that project, but I would have been very *much* happier with my writing since that time. I think I've learned a lot about how to write a little bit better."

[89] Rose: "I would hope they would say that it was clear. And I hope, what's really important to me is that whatever I'm writing about, that I thoroughly look at the subject matter whether it someone's story or something from history or its a subject—I don't ever want to treat that lightly. And I hope they can see the effort to put towards that in my writing. And the concern that I have for the topic or for the person."

[90] Jesse: "I've come to recognize that as a gift from God specifically for ministry and for life and I try to use my writing to build others up and to serve others because I find I can in writing

God's call to write flows the drives to read, to master the craft, to embrace vulnerability, and to live a fully integrated life. And all of this is done, not for our glory, but to build up the church. Robin said it well:

> Communication is a gift. And it's a gift you can offer to others. Investing in that gift is part of your calling while you're a student. You may think, "I'm not going to write again." but you will communicate. And you may have to write newsletters, or you may be preaching sermons, or you may be writing something more substantial. There are different ways of communicating and by focusing on your writing and investing in becoming the clearest communicator you can, you're offering a gift to the church.

What about the Prophetic Voice?

It made sense, given the seminary context, to find writers who saw their writing in terms of a pastoral call. But it was surprising, again given the context, not to find anyone speak of writing in terms of the prophetic voice. After all, the prophetic voice is based in the long tradition of the biblical prophets. Abraham Joshua Heschel, in his book *The Prophets* explains it this way,

> The prophet is a man who feels fiercely. God has thrust a burden upon his soul, and he is bowed and stunned at man's fierce greed. Frightful is the agony of man; no human voice can convey its full terror. Prophecy is the voice that God has lent to the silent agony, a voice to the plundered poor, to the profaned riches of the world. It is a form of living, a crossing point of God and man. God raging in the prophet's words.[91]

I can say things that I just can't otherwise. I just really tried to write in a way that is glorifying to God because I see it as worship not just because I've been given its primary purpose is to glorify God to build up my relationship with Christ.

[91] Abraham J. Heschel, *The Prophets* (New York: Harper Perennial Modern Classics, 2001), 5-6.

The prophetic voice in writing is that voice which beholds the world with clear eyes and whose heart cannot be still. The prophet speaks truth to power. It is the ability to look at something and say, "This is not the way things are supposed to be!" To stand on the proverbial street corner and use your words to shake things up, to make a scene, to ruffle feathers, rock the boat, roar like a lion. Anne Lamott says it this way,

> We write to expose the unexposed. If there is one door in the castle you have been told not to go through, you must. Otherwise, you'll just be rearranging furniture in rooms you've already been in. Most human beings are dedicated to keeping that one door shut. But the writer's job is to see what's behind it, to see the bleak unspeakable stuff, and to turn the unspeakable into words—not just into any words but if we can, into rhythm and blues.[92]

The prophetic is often the voice from the margins. The prophet is not overly concerned with stability, security, and the status quo, in fact, she is often looking to upset these things. Which is perhaps why this element did not show up in the research. It is not that students and faculty do not have anything to say about injustice, but that they feel the risk of ruffling the wrong feathers. Usually prophets are unpopular. Prophetic students risk their grade, while prophetic professors risk tenure and rank within the institution.

It is also significant that all research participants were—as are the majority of students and faculty—white Protestants. In America, the strongest prophetic voices in America have come from people of color like James Baldwin, Martin Luther King Jr., Maya Angelou, Toni Morrison; writers who offered a story that the world was not always ready to hear. Cornel West spoke about his writing,

---

[92] Lamott, 198.

I look at the world through the lens of the cross. That means I always start with the catastrophic. The horrendous, the scandalous, the monstrous...In America, you talk about the catastrophic, you talk about what? Indigenous people, slavery, women and patriarchy and domestic violence leaving scars. You talk about gay brothers and lesbian sisters taught to hate themselves. Talk about workers crushed by capitalist elites. It's the view from the bottom, up. It's the view through the lens of the cross. And that view is always a minority view within the Christian community.[93]

Surely the demographics of the context are significant. If the student (or faculty) population contained more voices that are typically marginalized, including women, racial minorities, or LGBTQ students, it might increase the chance of finding people who see the world and their writing through "the lens of the cross."

But this raises another question: could an institution like a seminary be a place that fosters the prophetic voice in its students and faculty? Or do institutions require a level of cohesiveness within its body in order to function? Can the prophetic ever be *allowed?* Or does permission negate the prophetic voice? What is the difference between prophetic and petulant? Can the Christian writer write prophetically while depending on the institution (school or church) for promotion, certification, or livelihood?

One faculty, who did not participate in the initial research and who wished not to be named, believed there were ways an institution could develop the prophetic voice within itself, and that some theological schools were already doing this, saying that, "A number of theological schools have fostered the prophetic voice across their institutions through programs, curricula, pedagogies,

[93] YouTube. "Writers On Writing with Cornel West (Part 1)." November 10, 2010. Accessed September 16, 2015. https://www.youtube.com/watch?v=TiJGCUKW5xk.

hiring, careful admissions processes…through incorporating cultural competency into the certificate of fitness process, and by incentivizing current faculty to write and teach with a more prophetic voice."[94] It is messy to encourage and develop critical voices, but doing so is not a secondary issue. Fredrick Buechner summed up the importance of the prophetic voice,

> One wonders if there is anything more crucial for the preacher to do than to obey the sadness of our times by taking it into account without equivocation or subterfuge, by speaking out of our times and into our times not just what we ought to say about the Gospel, not just what it would appear to be in the interests of the Gospel for us to say, but what we have ourselves felt about it, experienced of it. It is possible to think of the Gospel and our preaching of it as, above all and at no matter what risk, a speaking of the truth about the way things are.[95]

Good Christian writers are people who read, write, and embrace vulnerability. They write with their whole selves and try to be pastoral as they do. These seemingly simple tasks are actually a complicated blend of time management, technical mastery, and personal integrity. Good writing seems effortless, but is a struggle. At times it can feel overwhelming.

Therefore the question becomes: are there ways to improve in any of these areas? How does a person, practically speaking, set about to write from a place of integration? Can you learn to write pastorally? Can you improve your ability to read well? What is the most effective way to hone your craft? Can we learn to identify writing that is ill-informed, sloppy, defensive, over-intellectualized, and

---

[94] Personal correspondence.

[95] Frederick Buechner, *Telling the Truth: the Gospel as Tragedy, Comedy, and Fairy Tale* (San Francisco: Harper & Row, 1977), 7.

mean-spirited? Is there space to evaluate a piece of writing, not only by its technical prowess or adherence to orthodoxy, but by the criteria of hospitality, even as it offers a prophetic word? In the next chapter we will explore what should be happening when a Christian sits down to write.

Chapter Three:

Is There a Christian Writing Process?

What happens when a Christian sits down to write? Is there anything different happening from when a non-Christian does the same? For example, does being a Christian limit what subjects are permissible? Is a Christian required to maintain an orthodox point of view? Or, on the positive side, does the support of a church community provide the needed encouragement that allows a Christian writer to take more risks? If, as we have seen in the previous chapter, a good Christian writer is supposed to pay attention, live whole-heartedly, embrace vulnerability, and speak a prophetic word—*how do they do this*?

The answer depends, of course, on your understanding of what are the "best practices" with regard to the writing process. In truth, among the variety of opinions, the best process is the one that works for you—the one that produces the best writing. Yet, for the purposes of this paper, we will ground our understanding in the work of Peter Elbow. Peter Elbow is one of the most influential thinkers in regard to effective ways to teach the writing process. A teacher at the University of Massachusetts Amherst and Director of the school's Writing Program, his written work includes, *Writing Without Teachers, Writing with Power, Everyone Can Write,* and *Vernacular Eloquence.* The major themes of his work include the role of unbridled free-writing, reader-based feedback, and participatory teaching. Many of his ideas are now integrated into most methodologies of writing instruction. He has influenced numerous writers and teachers, many of whom will also be referenced.

Similarly, just as it depends on where we locate ourselves within the conversation about writing pedagogy, it also matters where we locate ourselves within 'best practices' of the Christian faith. There is no need to go into the various disagreements and schisms the Church has suffered trying to figure out what it means to be a faithful follower of Christ. But for our purposes, how we understand the Christian faith must be broad enough to include practices that the majority of Christians would recognize as, if not essential, at least valuable. This is why I have drawn on beliefs and practices that are both catholic and historic.

The following is a list of the points of resonance between writing methodology and Christian faith. It is also a map for the remainder of this chapter. Only the final point—how the Lordship of Christ frees the Christian writer—has no cousin in writing pedagogy. The result is an understanding of writing that is akin to an act of faith, while also presenting a vision of faith that is more like a creative process rather than as a club to which we might belong.

Writing Practice	Spiritual Practice
Embodiment	Incarnation
Rest	Sabbath
Read Books	Indwell Scripture
Community	Church
Inspiration	Submission to the Holy Spirit

Embodiment and Incarnation

Good writing is filled with the sights, sounds, tastes, touches, smells, balances, tensions, relationships, and intricacies of life. Good writing crunches, crackles, bites, stings, and sings. Good writing replicates life with such clarity that readers nod their heads and think, "Isn't that how life is!" To do this, a writer will draw on the same elements that make life itself memorable: surprise, routine, detail, tenderness, connection, observation, and love. The more a writer is aware of their own experiences the greater their capacity for wrestling that life onto the page.

Yet, before they are writers, they are people—people who see, hear, taste, smell, and feel. They love, speak, fail, succeed, submit, and conquer. They laugh and weep, rejoice and endure, and finally, simply be.[96] A good writer tries to experience more of what the world has to offer because diverse experiences increases her ability to write with specificity of detail rather than cliché.[97]

---

[96] "All fiction is autobiography, because even that which we imagine is a collage of images and meanings that have come into, and have been transformed by, our minds. Fiction is *an autobiography of the imagination.*" Pat Schneider, *Writing Alone and with Others* (Oxford: Oxford University Press, 2003) 138.

[97] "Now to have things alive and interesting it must be personal, it must come from the "I": what *I* know and feel. For that is the only great and interesting thing. That is the only truth *you* know, that nobody else does." Brenda Ueland, *If You Want to Write: A Book about Art, Independence and Spirit* (St. Paul: Greywolf Press, 1938) 71.

Yet, adding experience isn't about gathering data, or checking things off a list, or capturing moments in time. It's about becoming a better person.[98] A good writer strives to become more comfortable with herself because *who she is* will bubble up and shine through her writing. If she is uncomfortable with herself, her reader is going to notice and be uncomfortable with her too.

Being "comfortable in your own skin" is both metaphorical and literal because writing is a full-bodied activity. It isn't just a mental exercise. It requires an awareness and use of every part of our selves.[99] Laraine Herring, in her book *Writing Begins with Breath: Embodying Your Authentic Voice,* writes about the idea, common among writers, that they can "live in their heads" and ignore their other parts.

> We must begin to make the connection between the authentic self and the physical form. Often, writers tend to live in their heads, with their bodies as convenient vehicles for transporting those heads. If we spend all our time in our heads, not only do we have to deal with all those messy thoughts spinning around, but we'll soon find ourselves seeking solutions to all our problems and navigating our lives through only one vehicle: the mind. The mind is not meant for all that work. The mind is a gigantic data

---

[98] "And that is why I have come to think that the only way to become a better writer is to become a better person. By better I do not mean goody-goodier, for a great person often does things that so-called good people think very bad indeed." Ueland, 129.

[99] "My general preparations include everything I do to be healthy and ready for surprises, with a full palette of resources available. I need energy to acquire skill, energy to practice, energy to keep going through the inevitable setbacks, energy to keep going when things look good and I am tempted to sit back and relax. I need physical energy, intellectual energy, libidinal energy, spiritual energy. The means to tapping these energies are well known: Exercise the body, eat well, sleep well, keep track of dreams, meditate, enjoy the pleasures of life, read and experience widely. When blocked, tap into the great block-busters: humor, friends, and nature." Stephen Nachmanovitch, *Free Play: The Power of Improvisation in Life and the Arts* (New York: Jeremy P Tarcher/Perigee Books, 1990) 74-75.

processor and can only work with the data it has in it, so creative solutions must come from outside the mind.[100]

Writers are not disembodied creatures typing out masterworks on spiritualized keyboards. People experience the world as bodies.[101] Therefore, we do not have bottomless time or energy at our disposal. We must stop to eat, sleep, commune with others, relieve ourselves, and step outside to breathe some fresh air. Matthew 26:41 says, "The mind is willing, but the flesh is weak." This leads some Christians to divide the mind from the body and believe that a "good" writer will use their strength of will to ignore, push aside, or blast through whatever physical limitation is blocking them. This belief places a premium on hard work, which can help writers meet deadlines, but does nothing to free them from the underlying fear—whether of their own insignificance or their inevitable death—that comes with being embodied creatures.

The positive side of this equation is that, as Herring states, "creative solutions must come from outside the mind." This means there can be non-writing solutions to writing problems. For example, suppose John is stuck in his writing. His impulse is to force the work, hoping his tenacity will break through the block. But when this doesn't work, he thinks about *other* areas of his life. He realizes that he's been busy with Christmas parties (and fatty foods) and buying presents

---

[100] Laraine Herring, *Writing Begins with Breath: Embodying Your Authentic Voice* (Boston: Shambhala Publications, Inc., 2007), 22.

[101] Even our minds are part of our bodies. Therefore, talking about the mind-body relationship is somewhat of a construct. We speak of emotions as belonging to the heart, but this metaphorical for they too belong to the mind. For further information on the mind-body connection read Daniel J. Siegel and Tina Payne Bryson, *The Whole-Brained Child: 12 Revolutionary Strategies to Nurture Your Child's Developing Mind* (New York: Bantam Books, 2012)

(with financial strain) and isn't sleeping much (or having sex with his wife). Seen this way, it's no wonder that his writing is stuck! When all the pieces of his life are laid out, he may find an easy solution (sleep, hydrate, eat more fiber, time with his wife) that frees him from his writing difficulties.

Christian theologians call embodiment *incarnation.* While there are Christians who view the body (flesh) as evil and the soul (spirit) as good,[102] there is a stronger biblical case supporting the belief that our bodies are part of what is means to be human. From Genesis 1-2, where God creates bodies and pronounces them "good," to the vision of our bodies—after returning to the dust—redeemed and renewed upon Christ's return,[103] incarnation is part of what it means to be human. To become fully human, Christ took on a body (Hebrews 2:14), and in so doing so, affirmed its goodness, both prior to his death and after the resurrection. [104] Jesus confirms this in his appearance to the two women named Mary (Matthew 28) and though his encouragement of his disciples to "Look at my hands and my feet. It is I myself! Touch me and see; a ghost does not have flesh and bones, as you see I have" (Luke 24:39, NIV).[105]

---

[102] Galatians 5: 16-17: "So I say, walk by the Spirit, and you will not gratify the desires of the flesh. For the flesh desires what is contrary to the Spirit, and the Spirit what is contrary to the flesh. They are in conflict with each other, so that you are not to do whatever you want."
[103] "Not only so, but we ourselves, who have the firstfruits of the Spirit, groan inwardly as we wait eagerly for our adoption as sons, the redemption of our bodies." (NIV)

[104] "Jesus was, in Max Weber's terminology, both an ethical prophet - one who outlines rules of conduct for his followers - and an exemplary prophet - one who presents his own life as an example to his followers." Ron Hansen, *A Stay Against Confusion: Essays on Faith and Fiction* (New York: HarperCollins Publishers, 2001) 22.

[105] For further reading on embodiment, consider Henri de Lubac's, *Catholicism: Christ and the Common Destiny of Man* (San Francisco: Ignatius Press, 1988)

Therefore, Christian writers can accept their own bodies—with their limits—as a gift from God. They can begin to see their writing in holistic terms. They should apply Christ's instruction to, "Love the Lord your God with all your heart and with all your soul and with all your strength and with all your mind" (Luke 10:27) to their writing. Poet Luci Shaw writes about how God anticipated the human impulse to over-intellectualize life,

> God, who knows us better than we know ourselves, isn't content to speak simply to the rational intelligence but informs us through beauty, imagination, and intuition. Where doctrinal principles seem logical, though abstract, images print themselves on our minds and even on our sense in such brilliant color and three-dimensional texture that time and distraction cannot obliterate them.[106]

The writing process of the embodied Christian will include working on their craft, expanding their vocabulary, and studying plot and structure. But it will also include getting enough sleep, eating well, drinking enough water, breathing deeply, practicing solitude, managing stress, maintaining healthy sexual relationships, and keeping in touch with family and friends. By doing these things—by becoming more aware of our interior life and the world around us—we affirm the goodness of creation and increase our capacity to live creatively.

But the equation runs both ways. If we practice being creative in holistic and integrative ways, then other aspects of our life will shift and change. Virginia Hampton Wright explains the interconnectedness of engaging creatively when she writes,

> You can't engage with a creative process and not engage other processes. When you are exploring and unveiling, your emotions get hooked, your intellect gets hooked, and your deepest beliefs

---

[106] Luci Shaw, *Breath for the Bones: Art, Imagination, and Spirit: Reflections on Creativity and Faith* (Nashville: Thomas Nelson, 2007) 9.

about life get hooked. If creativity is nurtured well and allowed to grow, it will grab onto your life in multiple ways.[107]

Fortunately, there's an historic Christian practice that recognizes the implications of human embodiment and it's one that the aspiring writer can borrow: observing the Sabbath.

Rest and Sabbath

Many people struggle to find time to write. If someone suggested *rest* as the solution to their writing problem, they would respond with incredulity. They might push back, "I can't even find five minutes a day to write! And you are telling me to rest? The problem is that I rest too much!"

But this confuses *not writing* with resting. It may be true that they are not writing, but they're spending energy on work, television, kids, friends, hobbies, social media, volunteering, cooking, and cleaning the house. When the time comes to write they are tired, distracted, and uninspired. Trying to write without first accepting that you really need rest and recovery can pinch off your energy and leave you feeling guilty and hopeless.

Experienced writers (like experienced athletes) know that preparing to write is just as important as writing. Time and energy need to be curated and protected. After all, writing is a serious act and requires a serious effort. The infrastructure of our life—all our schedules and routines—creates the parameters

---

[107] Vinita Hampton Wright, *The Soul Tells a Story: Engaging Creativity with Spirituality in the Writing Life* (Downers Grove: InterVarsity Press, 2005) 20-21.

of our writing process. This is why Sabbath observance is powerful: because it structures our lives toward flourishing. Brenda Ueland was not addressing Sabbath observance in her wonderful book *So You Want to Write*, but still captures how not writing is a key part of the writing process.

> So [good writers] dare to be idle, i.e., not to be pressed and duty-driven all the time. They dare to love people even when they are very bad, and they dare not to try and dominate others to show them what they must do for their own good. For great and creative men know what is best for every man is his own freedom so that his imagination (it can also be called the conscience or the Holy Ghost) can grow in its own way, even if that way, to you or to me, or to policemen or churchgoers, seems very bad indeed.[108]

Ueland goes on to talk about the impulse to "grind" away at work—a term that captures the force, friction, and even violence that we inflict upon ourselves when we try to compel ourselves to do things that we are not prepared to do. However, good writing should have an easiness and freedom that works *with* rather than against our energies. In the same book Ueland writes,

> [S]top thinking of the creative power as nervous and effortful; in fact it can be frightened away by nervous straining. So never bother to grind. Just try to understand something for the time. If you don't, go on to the next. For if you understand the second or third thing, you will suddenly understand the first.[109]

In spite of the modern mantra to "work smarter, not harder," too often when writers are stuck they just push harder, work longer, and try to force something to happen. This method costs health, relationships, and happiness. Writing is often like quicksand: the more you struggle the more quickly you are doomed.

---

[108] Ueland, 30.
[109] Ueland, 47.

There are times to glue yourself to your chair and do the work. And yet, the best solution to "writer's block" might actually be to *let go*. Yield to the moment. Walk away. Stop struggling. Stop worrying. Stop even thinking about it. Take a nap or have lunch. Go have a drink with friends. When you return, what seemed opaque and foreboding is often clear and welcoming. Peter Elbow, in *Writing with Power* explains,

> The most effective way to deal with this frustrating case is of course to take a break. Put your writing away and forget about it for more than a day or two. You should be doing this periodically throughout revising. But there is another tactic that also helps: stop trying to solve the dilemma and simply *accept* it and *describe* it. Stop beating your head against the wall, stop pushing so hard against an immovable object, take the pressure off your shoulders. Pretend that things are just fine as they stand now, in their state of contradiction or confusion, and *describe* the conflicting details or ideas as accurately and happily as you can. This will often lead to new perspective and a solution.[110]

The idea that people should have both a time for work and a time for rest is part of Christianity's DNA, itself rooted in the Jewish understanding of Sabbath.[111] Abraham Joshua Heschel begins Chapter 1 of his book *The Sabbath* this way:

> He who wants to enter the holiness of the day must first lay down the profanity of clattering commerce, of being yoked to toil. He must go away from the screech of dissonant days, from the nervousness and fury of acquisitiveness and the betrayal in embezzling his own life. He must say farewell to manual work and learn to understand that the world has already been created and will survive without the help of man. Six days a week we wrestle with the world, wringing profit from the earth; on the Sabbath we especially care for the seed of eternity planted in the soul. The world has our hands, but our soul belongs to Someone Else. Six

---

[110] Peter Elbow, *Writing With Power,* (New York: Oxford University Press, 1981) 133.

[111] Ecclesiastes 3:1 There is a time for everything, and a season for every activity under the heavens.

days a week we seek to dominate the world, on the seventh day we try to dominate the self.[112]

Still, the Christian writer should not see Sabbath observance as the "silver bullet" to making him or her a great writer. While resting once a week might have the effect of raising productivity, Sabbath is not primarily a productivity technique. It is not a necessary evil to accommodate the limits of human embodiment. It is the highest day, the day when we are most ourselves, later in the same book Heschel writes,

> To the biblical mind, however, labor is the means toward an end, and the Sabbath as a day of rest, as a day of abstaining from toil, is not for the purpose of recovering one's lost strength and becoming fit for the forthcoming labor. The Sabbath is a day for the sake of life. Man is not a beast of burden, and the Sabbath is not for the purpose of enhancing the efficiency of his work.[113]

Still, we do well to remember Jesus' words in Mark 2 when confronted about why his disciples were not being zealous in their observation of Sabbath law, "The Sabbath is made for man, not man for the Sabbath. So the Son of Man is Lord even of the Sabbath." In this verse Christians are challenged to evaluate their Sabbath theology through the words of Christ. It might be, that due to overly busy weeks, taking time to write could becomes a way to *observe* the Sabbath and experience its blessings.

Read Books and Indwell Scripture

---

[112] Abraham Joshua Heschel, *The Earth is the Lords* & *The Sabbath* (New York: Harper Torchbooks) 1966, 13.

[113] Heschel, *Sabbath,* 14.

Every writer is first a reader.[114] This is how people start writing: they read a book and think, "I want to try that." Voluminous reading is common and solid writing advice. Yann Martel said,

> The key thing I would say to anyone who aspires to write would be to read. The best teacher is a cheap little Penguin Classic. Read beyond what you want to write. So if you want to write romance, great, but also read science fiction, read classics. If you aspire to be a literary writer, if you aspire to be the next John Updike, read Harlequins. Read beyond the narrow ken of what you particularly like. Read. Read. Read.[115]

Reading is an intimate activity. It turns your mental processes over to another person. You see things they want you to see. You hear sounds not really present. You even feel emotions not originally yours. All of this affects a writer. The books you have read are always inside you, mingling with your own thoughts and language. The long-term immersion in quality writing raises a writer's vocabulary, standards, and level of taste. It builds the library of images and characters available to a writer, and therefore adds a level of intention with regard to creating layers of meaning. It also provides a deeper understanding of the context into which a writer's work falls.

In fact, for some writers, reading takes priority over writing. Cornel West sees his writing as a participation in and reaction to what he reads.[116] Annie

---

[114] "Reading, the love of reading, is what makes you dream of becoming a writer. And long after you've become a writer, reading books others write — and rereading the beloved books of the past — constitutes an irresistible distraction from writing. Distraction. Consolation. Torment. And, yes, inspiration." Susan Sontag, *"Directions: Writer, Read, Repeat. Repeat Steps 2 and 3 as Needed," New York Times,* December 18, 2000, accessed September 18, 2013, http://www.nytimes.com/2000/12/18/arts/18SONT.html

[115]Yann Martel, *Learning How To Write Well*, accessed October 15, 2013, http://youtu.be/IR9Av-TzSV4

Dillard says that reading is essential for the writer because it is, "Only after the writer lets literature shape her can she perhaps shape literature."[117] And Joyce Carol Oates says that,

> Young or beginning writers must be urged to read widely, ceaselessly, both classics and contemporaries, for without an immersion in the history of the craft, one is doomed to remain an amateur: an individual for whom enthusiasm is ninety-nine percent of the creative effort.[118]

What drives such fervor for reading is the understanding that all writing is, in some way, a response to what has come before. It may not always seem that way, especially if we are unaware of the wider literary conversations, but this is why it is important that writers be aware of the traditional forms, historical progressions, schools of thought, and current trends.[119]

In *How to Read Literature Like a Professor,* Thomas C. Foster expounds on this concept in the chapter titled "When in Doubt, It's From Shakespeare." He outlines the influence that Shakespeare has had on English literature, not only through the Bard's own work, but through the subsequent response, integration, and reimagining of authors like William Faulkner, Jane Smiley, Aldous Huxley,

---

[116] "54 year old black man in America and I never understood myself first and foremost as a writer....Toni Morrison, who I love...Toni Morrison is a writer, you know why? Because every morning she gets up, she writes...Whereas for me, I read. I'm first and foremost a reader. My writing is just a by-product. It's a conversation with what I'm reading with, in order to teach!" Writers on Writing with Cornel West (Part 1), accessed October 16, 2013, http://youtu.be/TiJGCUKW5xk

[117] Annie Dillard, *The Writing Life* (New York: Harper & Row Publishers, 1989), 69.

[118] Joyce Carol Oates, *The Faith of a Writer: Life, Craft, Art* (New York: Harper Collins, 2003), xii.

[119] "But real learning, in contrast, is the phenomenon of so abundantly "understanding" the concepts in the book or lecture that it becomes part of us and determines the way we see, feel, and act - the way we process the widest range of data." Elbow, *Embracing Contraries*: *Explorations in Learning and Teaching*, (New York, Oxford University Press, 1986), 13.

Ray Bradbury, and T.S. Eliot. Each of these people reacted to something Shakespeare wrote. (Or reacted to reactions.) So a familiarity of the work of Shakespeare will allow the writer to enter into the inter-textual conversations that are always going on. Foster writes,

> This dialogue between old texts and new is always going on at one level or another. Critics speak of this dialogue as *intertextuality*, the ongoing interaction between poems or stories. This intertextual dialogue deepens and enriches the reading experience, bringing multiple layers of meaning to the text, some of which readers may not even consciously notice. The more we become aware of the possibility that our text is speaking to other texts, the more similarities and correspondences we begin to notice, and the more alive the text becomes.[120]

The writer gains a valuable tool if she is familiar with Shakespeare, but not only Shakespeare, but also with the literary canon. Similarly, the more widely she reads *outside* the canon the more images, plots, characters, scenes, and twist she will be able to use or adapt. After all, all writing is reinvention and there is very little that is original. What she takes in will be what she puts out. Reading is the ink in the writer's pen.

An advantage for the Christian writer is that the Bible has had at least as significant an influence on English literature as Shakespeare. In fact, Foster follows his chapter "When in Doubt, It's from Shakespeare…" with one titled, "…or the Bible." Similar to Shakespeare, the Bible—as literature—has influenced writers such as John Steinbeck, Toni Morrison, James Joyce, John Milton and myriad others.

---

[120] Thomas C. Foster, *How to Read Literature Like a Professor: A Lively and Entertaining Guide to Reading Between the Lines* (New York: Harper Perennial, 2003), 29.

This is how a Christian writer has an advantage over a non-Christian writer: greater familiarity with the original stories (Creation, Cain and Abel, Noah's Ark, Sacrifice of Isaac, David and Goliath, etc.) and texts (Sermon on the Mount, Miracles of Christ, teachings of Paul) that have shaped English literature in significant ways. Consider these titular examples: *Absalom, Absalom* (Faulkner), *East of Eden* (Steinbeck), *Song of Solomon* (Morrison), *A Time to Kill* (Grisham), *Gilead* (Robinson), *Number the Stars* (Lowry), *Jacob have I Loved* (Patterson), *In the Beginning* (Potok). Each of these stories stand alone, but are enriched by knowing the biblical allusion.

However, for the Christian writer, the Bible is not just a literary text akin to *Hamlet* but it is scripture. It points us beyond ourselves and tells us about God. Foster concisely articulates the role the Bible has played as literature, but he ignores the influence it has had on writers' beliefs. To the Christian, scripture is not like other books. And while there is disagreement about what scripture is and isn't, everyone agrees there is something special about it. It is not mere coincidence that the stories of the Bible have become the forms we use for our stories. Luci Shaw explains that,

> As artists, what we look for in making the connections, what we need, and what the Holy Spirit gave in inspiring the biblical writers are images that work. The more effective and varied the images, the more levels of truth and illumination they provide. We need multiplicity; the more images the better, not mixed but compounded. What one images fails to recognize, another will pick up, like the reflection seen in different facets of a gem as it is turned in the light.[121]

---

[121] Shaw, 15.

Whatever a Christian writer might feel about the Bible, whatever criticism can be leveled against it as patriarchal, culturally bound, or antiquated, she should not stop engaging with the biblical text. Christian writers have been arguing about, wrestling with, and disagreeing over the meaning of Scripture ever since there *was* Scripture. What we read shapes who we are, and who we are will bubble up in our writing, therefore a Christian writer should read the Bible.[122]

Of course, a person *can* be a great writer without knowledge of either Shakespeare or the Bible. So too, someone can be a wonderful Christian without deep biblical training. But the Christian writer who neglects her relationship with Scripture will be short-changing herself, both as a writer and a follower of Christ. C.S. Lewis held a high view of both literature and Scripture and regularly communed with both. Luci Shaw writes about him,

> It was Lewis's conviction...that if we saturate ourselves in richly creative literature—in Scripture with its potent imagery; in fiction with its narrative flow and power; in poetry that joins emotion with idea, image, and music, logic with intuition, and proposition with imaginative truth—that division may be healed and unity restored.[123]

But this "saturation" in Scripture and great literature should not be done alone. It is an activity best done with other people.

Community and the Church

---

[122] "I have found that as I allow the created universe and the ingrained Scripture to illuminate me, what I deeply believe pushes up through the fabric of words, often in the most surprising and unplanned way." Shaw, 63-64.

[123] Shaw, 71.

69

As we grow from children to adults, we gain independence. This is healthy and necessary. But when independence metastasizes it hardens into individualism. Right now, America has stage-four individualism. It begins in early elementary school when we start to evaluate children, not as a group, but as a collection of individuals. In fact, the idea of grading a group of students *as a whole* would incite parents to riot. And to be fair, who hasn't felt the bitterness (or sweetness, depending) of being part of a group project where a few people did the majority of the work?

However, recognizing our dependency on those around us might not only better reflect the reality of both childhood and adulthood, it may, in fact, be the best way to encourage learning, human flourishing, and appropriate interdependence. Peter Elbow, in *Embracing Contraries: Explorations in Learning and Teaching* writes how,

> So many parents and teachers fear allowing a student to have an acknowledged dependency. We reward children and students for being autonomous and separated—unmerged with authority figures—from the earliest possible age. In this way too, we bamboozle them and prevent them from growing: making them think their problem is lack of courage to be autonomous and self-actualized. They are all doing push-ups trying to develop the "courage to be free," when what so many of them lack is the courage to be dependent, the courage to be unfree.[124]

Of course, writing is a solitary act. A person sits down with paper and pen or at a computer and begins to write. This can lead people to believe that writers are "lone wolf" types. And yet, while that particular part of the writing process *is*

---

[124] Elbow, *Embracing Contraries,* 97.

done alone, this does not mean that writers are necessarily introverted, isolated, or don't need people to be involved in *other* parts of their writing process.

In fact, a writer will benefit from participation in a community, not only because writers are people and people need community, but because writing is an act of vulnerability.[125] First, the writing process requires exposing yourself to…*yourself.* Writing often asks a writer to come face-to-face with his limits, abilities, and muddled thinking. Without a group of people to provide love and encouragement, without a safe place to test-run ideas before sharing them with a wider audience, writers can find themselves paralyzed by fear. Meeting regularly with people (or even one person) can provide accountability, hope, and affirmation. If your community contains other writers you will also be able to solicit technical feedback on issues like argument, plot, structure, and grammar.[126]

However, finding a good writing community can be hard to do.[127] Writing groups are not always the healthiest environments. Depending on the leadership

---

[125] Behind the reticence and sense of being gagged lies a need to be genuinely listened to, to carry some weight, to make a dent. I want a chance for my words to penetrate to a level of serious consciousness." Elbow, *Embracing Contraries,* 83.

[126] "Most of us have had a teacher or reader who made us want to write - and unfortunately, also, the opposite kind. The safe reader gave us a kind of attention that somehow made us feel respected, taken seriously, and supported, and as a result, we usually ended up having more and better things to say that we had expected. Because I call him safe I don't mean to say such a reader is always gentle and soft. Some safe readers are tough and demanding but they listen hard, they respect us, they want to hear what we have to say, and in this way they bring out our best skills in writing. The unsafe reader makes us feel that we don't count or that our words are irrelevant and makes it harder than usual for us not only to think of things to write, but also to put down on paper what we already have in mind." Elbow, *Writing with Power,* 185

[127] "Another reason we stay isolated is that we don't have a firm grasp ourselves of our creative process. Because we have not truly said yes to the work, or we haven't submitted to the process in an intentional way, or we haven't developed the practices we need, we are easily threatened by outside forces. When we're barely hanging on to a sense of our creative gifts, the last thing we want is to be thrust into a community that may or may not understand or help us develop them." Hampton Wright, 142-143.

and the members they can actually damage and destroy rather than build up. But while it may take time, writing groups can be instructive. Elbow writes:

> When you hear someone read a piece every week or two, someone no better than you, and you see her come up with a passage that is terrific—but she's using the same old ingredients that she and you have been struggling with week after week—sometimes you learn more about how to improve your writing than you learn from clear explanations of what is wrong with it or good advice about how to fix it, or inspiring lectures on the seven essentials of good writing.[128]

And it is worth noting that a writing group is not something that is useful to a point—something that helps you become a success but is then cast aside. Pat Scheinder in the wonderful *Writing Alone and With Others* writes:

> Once I sat at lunch with a writer who had been awarded a Pulitzer Prize. He said in an anguished voice, "What in the world can I write to follow a Pulitzer?" The fear of success, perhaps as much as the fear of failure, may block our art. The successful writer, no less than the beginner, needs the consolation and support of a community of writing friends.[129]

It isn't just writers, but all people—Christians and non-Christians alike—who need "the consolation and support of a community of writing friends." But the Christian is likely already part of a community: the church.

The church has been the community of Christian believers for 2000 years.[130] In fact, while it is true that many Christians understand their faith in

---

[128] Elbow, *Writing with Power*, 23.

[129] Scheinder, *Writing Alone and With Others*, 16.

[130] Unfortunately, churches have not always supported the arts, or artists. There have be periods in history when Christian artists and storytellers were some of the best and the brightest. But the current state of Christian writing often separates writing into categories of "religious" and "secular." And yet, just because the formal structures of the church has not, or does not, encouraged the creative arts, it does not mean that there are not people within the walls of the church who could offer you love and support in your writing.

terms of an individual relationship to God, there is an inherently communal aspect to Christianity. Virginia Hampton Wright, in *The Soul Tells a Story: Engaging Creativity with Spirituality in the Writing Life* writes how,

> From my earliest days it was ingrained in my thinking—by Scriptures, hymns and liturgies—that we're all part of one community. The New Testament book of 1 Corinthians talks at length about what that means. I assume that if one person in my community suffers, all of us do. I believe that I share responsibility for the lives of people everywhere, if only through my prayers and my manner of life on this earth. I operate out of the worldview that I am irrevocably connected to other humans regardless of how well I know or like them, and vice versa.[131]

Further, the Christian writer also writes in relationship to God and to humanity. Bret Lott, in *Letters & Life: On Being a Writer, On Being a Christian,* writes about how Christians cannot forget their relationship to wider society. "[W]e do not commit art in a vacuum but are a part of society—of humanity—at large, and therefore we indeed have a role in that society, a role that can and will contribute to the harmonization of human activity at large. We have been blessed to be a blessing."[132]

However, the dynamic of any group is always towards its own survival, even if it must destroy some of its members. So a writer must balance loyalty to the group with faithfulness to their creative vision. This is true in a writing group *and* in a church.[133] There are Christians who feel most comfortable within

---

[131] Hampton Wright, 142.

[132] Bret Lott, *Letters & Life: On Being a Writer, On Being a Christian* (Wheaton: Crossway, 2013) 34.

[133] "I am trying to broaden our conception of thinking or purposive rationality. Instead of characterizing it as a single effort in more or less one direction, I portray it as the interaction between two efforts in two conflicting directions. That is, instead of seeing rationality as primarily the attempt to make inferences that are careful and conscious, I portray it as the interaction

orthodoxy, tradition, dogma, and accepted polity. These people will be suspicious if anyone steps outside these bounds. Similarly, there are secular writers who argue that, as artists, the only allegiance should be to the art. This group can be dismissive of talking about their responsibility for the social impact of their work. But a Christian writer who participates in community does not have the luxury to choose sides in this equation, because sometimes their work will come out of, and be aimed back toward, their own community. (This is the prophetic voice that was explained in the previous chapter.)

Christian writers have a responsibility to the community to which they belong. They also have a responsibility to their art. Therefore they need to be both faithful to the message within them *and* to consider the impact of what they write. Truth can both hurt and help, and sometimes it's difficult to know which is which. But Christians do not have the secular artist's luxury to ignore the effect of their work. They may stir the pot, but they should do so with intention. They should not try to break down, but to build up—even if from the outside[134] it looks like the same thing.[135]

---

between that attempt and a contrary one—sometimes thought of as *non*rational—toward association, digression, and the relinquishing of control. In short, the contrary I'm interested in here is that between *careful* and *careless* thinking - the process of learning how to move back and forth between imposing control and relinquishing it." Elbow, *Embracing Contraries*, 54.

[134] "Your willingness to grapple with questions will unnerve people who banned serious questions from their life years ago. Your tendency to bump into dark, shadowy things will convince some people that you're losing your religious bearings; their religious practice has been to avoid dealing with any darkness at all, beyond labeling as evil anything that makes them uncomfortable." Hampton Wright, 29.

[135] Michael "I think for me it's a space that is *trying* to nurture discipleship in a creative way. Is trying to open up a more expansive vision of what God is doing. And if I have to criticize people on the way, I will do it, but I'll try to do it graciously in a way that isn't *ad hominem* and that sort of thing. And obviously isn't arising from trying to get back at a person. Sometimes that's necessary on the task of trying helping people have a more expansive vision. But I would say, in a

And this gets to a further point about community. A writer might speak a word of truth, but then the community gets to speak back, gets a chance to respond to the work.[136] The writer has a responsibility to their community, not necessarily to toe the party line, but at least to share their work and give others a chance to respond. This is true for all people, regardless of their faith. Pat Schneider argues,

> When we write, we create, and when we offer our creation to one another, we close the wound of loneliness and may participate in healing the broken world. Our words, our truth, our imagining, our dreaming, may be the best gifts we have to give.[137]

Inspiration and Submission to the Holy Spirit

There is something mysterious about writing. Stepping out onto the blank page is an act of faith even for the most worldly. Speaking at the *Festival of Faith and Writing,* Katherine Paterson said most colorfully: "Tonight I promised to talk

---

word, a more expansive vision of the Kingdom. A more expansive vision of what God is doing. And it's that positive constructive task which has got to drive it. So if I have…to deconstruct something, but I refuse to deconstruct without reconstructing, without giving an alternative vision that takes seriously the ministry concerns and tries to make a case for a more expansive positive vision."

[136] "When people are stubborn and narrow-minded, they refuse to allow the material in their head to be restructured by what the other person says: they simply hang on to the orientations they have and are too afraid to relinquish any of them." Peter Elbow, *Writing Without Teachers,* 2nd ed. (New York: Oxford University Press, 1998) 50.

[137] Schneider, xix

about the imagination, but like many writers, I have a sort of spooky feeling that if I start dissecting the creative process to see what makes it hop, I may very well end up with a dead frog."[138]

What happens in the writing process is often unknown even to its most experienced practitioners.[139] C.S. Lewis wrote that,

> You must not believe all that authors tell you about how they wrote their books. This is not because they mean to tell lies. It is because a man writing a story is too excited about the story itself to sit back and notice how he is doing it. In fact, that might stop the work, just as, if you start thinking about how you tie your tie, the next thing is that you find you can't tie it. And afterwards, when the story is finished, he has forgotten a good deal of what writing it was like.[140]

And not to belabor the point, but John Steinbeck said of writing, "We work in our own darkness a great deal with little real knowledge of what we are doing. I think I know better what I am doing than most writers but it still isn't much."[141]

Even someone like Peter Elbow, who has studied writing instruction for decades, still leaves room for the mysterious. He has seen first-hand how many

---

[138] Katherine Paterson in *Shouts and Whispers: Twenty-One Writers Speak about their Writing and their Faith*, ed. Jennifer L. Holberg (Grand Rapids: William B. Eerdmans Publishing Co., 2006) 13.

[139] What prevents most people from being inventive and creative is fear of looking foolish. After all, if you just let words and ideas come out without checking them first, some may indeed be stupid. But when you know that this is just the first of two stages, and that you are getting more and more critical in the second stage, you feel safer writing freely, tapping intuition, and going out on limbs. You will be more creative." Elbow, *Writing with Power,* 10.

[140] C.S. Lewis, *Of Other Worlds: Essays and Stories*, ed. Walter Hooper (New York: Harcourt, Brace & World Inc., 1966), 42.

[141] John Steinbeck, "The Art of Fiction, No. 45," *The Paris Review,* No. 63 (Fall 1975) accessed October 16, 2013.

writers cannot handle the mess of the mystery and who attempt to write perfectly on their first draft. To these people (and to all who wish to write) he advocates,

> Practice letting the process itself decide what happens next—decide, for example, whether your focusing sentence springboards you into a new treatment of the same material, into a response to that material or into some other new topic or mode that "wants" to come next. If it sounds a bit mystical to say "Let it decide," I don't mean to rule out hard conscious thinking. "Letting it decide" will often mean realizing you should be rigorously logical at this point in the writing cycle. As you practice the open-ended writing process, you will get better at feeling what kind of step needs to be taken at any given point. The main thing is not to worry about doing it right. Just do it a lot.[142]

And it is around this idea where writing has most of its mystery. After all, most children can put words on paper and most high school students can apply the basic rules of grammar and structure. But how it all comes together, and from where the ideas originate, *that* is often a mystery.

For the Christian (truthfully, for anyone) to abandon the higher faculties can be very frightening. Christians pride themselves on self-control and personal discipline. In most Protestant and Catholic traditions the more Pentecostal, mystical, or ecstatic elements are often marginalized. To uncouple themselves from judgment and discernment would be to ask most Christians to step into an unknown world.

Yet acting without an assurance of what will result should be a natural thing for Christians. This is faith. It is stepping out onto the voice of God, and it happens in the Bible from beginning to end: Abraham, Moses, Esther, Elijah, Mary, Jesus, Peter, and Paul. Each of these people had to act without certainty.

---

[142] Peter Elbow, *Writing Without Teachers*, 2nd ed. (New York: Oxford University Press, 1998), 53.

And we share their condition. Vinita Wright Hampton assesses the situation well when she writes:

> When you open up to life at its fullest, you may feel a little giddy.
> Actually, you may be filled with sheer terror. Learning to be open
> is not easy, for you or for some of the people around you.
> Openness subjects you to the unknown, and often the most
> religiously minded people have trouble with that. We turn to
> religious belief for many reasons, and a major reason is our desire
> for safety. Well, openness does not enhance a feeling of safety,
> which is why openness alone is not enough…When you are
> submitting, in faith, to that divine process and the God who
> oversees it, you can afford to be open.[143]

So too, the writing process requires a level of faith. Not only must a writer trust that they will not lose heart and abandon their project, but also that the words will keep coming, that they will find a sensible form, and their audience will receive the work as intended.

When a non-Christian says that they need to "trust the process," what they mean is that they hope things turn out well, even though they have no reason to believe they will. But when a Christian says that they need to trust the process, they are saying that the results of their effort are not theirs to evaluate. Instead, faithfulness to the call is what matters. When done in faith, the results belong to God.[144]

Furthermore, Christians who understand *sin* and *grace* should be better suited to let go of control.[145] For where the non-Christian writer has to trust

---

[143] Hampton Wright, 92.

[144] "Love God and do whatever you please: for the soul trained in love to God will do nothing to offend the One who is Beloved." Augustine of Hippo.

[145] "Fullness of life in arenas of art and spirituality demands that we let go, that we relinquish control - something that goes against the human grain, particularly in a culture obsessed with empowerment. Here we are, trying to bring order and beauty out of chaos, gaining a kind of

themselves or "the muse" Christians confess that the Holy Spirit is alive and active in their hearts. It is this active, loving, and dependable entity that guides them. Luci Shaw derives much comfort from this as she writes her poetry.

> Faith is not linear. It is, indeed, that widening of the imagination, a leap into the transcendent, a taste of the numinous, the ability to see the extra ordinary in the ordinary. And our coach for the leap, the glue in the link, is the Spirit of God.[146]

Both writing and following Christ require practitioners to step into the unknown. When a writer attempts something with a vast scope and range, she must believe in her ability to write, that she will be able to hold the pieces together, and in her perseverance. When the person of faith attempts the same project, they have the benefit—however mysterious—of being guided by the Holy Spirit.

Do the Work and Accept the Call

There comes a time when all writers must begin the hard work of writing. After all, writing is serious work and should be approached seriously. Just like a professional musician or athlete, a writer must ready their body, mind, and as much as possible, their environment. Wishing will not put words on the page. Nor, in spite of all I have written thus far, can a person spend all their time trying to get healthy, read books, develop a community, or wait for inspiration. There

---

discipline and control, exercising the authority of experience and hard-won wisdom, and we have to *let it go*? How seemingly counterintuitive!" Shaw, 107.

[146] Shaw, 77.

are no ideal circumstances for writing so we cannot wait for them. It sounds obvious, but writers need to write.

And if a writer wants to create anything longer than a couple of pages—the amount that can be written in a single sitting—she is going to need personal discipline. The undisciplined writer will be overwhelmed by the staggering amount of work: the messy drafts, the rounds of editing, the rewrites, integrating feedback, and the poor odds of ever finding a place to publish. But the disciplined writer will balance realism and optimism.[147] She will divide her work into manageable chunks and recognize that pages add up and that a wall is built one brick at a time.

The disciplined writer will make the necessary sacrifices. For example, any person who claims that they will get up one hour earlier that usual in order to write is fooling themselves. It never works. First, because this takes time away from sleep, which is critical to good writing, and second, because writing cannot be an add-on to everything else in our lives. Writing requires that we make choices in how we use our time. It requires sacrifice.

Pat Schneider writes beautifully about her own epiphany about taking writing seriously or drifting along trying to do a little of this and a little of that,

> Suddenly I saw that I had to make a choice. I said to myself, you can't have it all. You have little time after parenting four children—you cannot crochet and preserve jellies and bake bread and make quilts and also write. The other forms of personal

---

[147] To be disciplined as a writer you need a compassionate and welcoming attitude toward your own work, and you need the support of others who value and call forth your writing. A huge part of leading a disciplined writing life is having other people in your life who care about your writing, want it, believe in it, and encourage it...Being a disciplined writing begins in your own mind." Schneider, 48-49.

expression are things I truly like to do, but that day I folded up the quilt pattern and scraps of cloth. I stopped making jelly; I gave up sewing forever. Because I wanted most to be a writer. I wanted to be an artist, and I knew I would have to be faithful to the practice of my art. I set up an office for myself in half a basement room and began (again) to write.[148]

So too, Christian writers are not exempt from time-management issues. They need to dedicate the same amount of hard work and personal discipline as any other writer. However, one possibly difference is that this work can spring from a sense of *gratitude*.[149] The Christian writer must be disciplined, but it is a discipline that is a response to love.[150] The order of these things is important: first the love, then the discipline. Christians should write not to *earn* love, but as a *response* to love. Discipline that flows out of love may look like the discipline that flows from anxiety, at least from the outside, but will feel differently and will result in different things.

The Christian writer understands that "all good and perfect gifts are from above" (James 1:17) and that any talent they have is a gift from God. Therefore, their actions should not be an attempt to win approval from their parents, society, or God. Instead, the Christian knows they are loved, just as they are. "It is by grace we have been saved, through faith" (Ephesians 2:8). Hard work should be a

---

[148] Schneider, 54.

[149] "We have come to think that duty should come first. I disagree. Duty should be a by-product. *Writing*, the creative effort, the use of the imagination, should come first,-at least for some part of every day of your life. It is a wonderful blessing if you will use it. You will become happier, more enlightened, alive, impassioned, lighthearted and generous to everybody else. Even your health will improve. Colds will disappear and all the other ailments of discouragement and boredom." Ueland, 14.

[150] "It is my deep conviction that true discipline is a matter of love, rather than duty. If you are in love, you make time and space for the believed. That preparation is part of the joy. There is nothing of duty about it. I believe that people who truly want to write are in love with writing, in love with the artist inside, in love with creating. That love is the root source of true discipline." Schneider, 51.

responsive act. Christians confess that we are already loved and worthy of love. This order is important because the risks and vulnerabilities of writing are just as real for the Christian writer as for the non-Christian.

A belief in an afterlife is another aid to the Christian writer. Christians understand themselves as eternal beings, to whom death does not mean the end of their identity, relationships, and even writing ability. Since how we use our time depends on how much time we believe we have left, the Christian writer can see their development in eschatological terms. It is not uncommon for writers to feel that they'll never have enough time to write all the books that they want to or that they aren't progressing fast enough or having the publishing success they desire. But remembering that life does not end with death can free the Christian writer from the pressure to accomplish everything right away and allow them to move forward at their own pace.

However, even with an eternity to write, the writing process still requires risk and vulnerability. Christians cannot escape this fact. But the Christian writer has one more thing that makes the risks more manageable: hope. Romans 8:24-26 says, "But hope that is seen is no hope at all. Who hopes for what they already have? But if we hope for what we do not yet have, we wait for it patiently. In the same way, the Spirit helps us in our weakness." In spite of the risks, the hard work, the disappointments, and the strain of wrestling meaning into words and then pinning them on the page, Christian writers can, out of gratitude, write with hope because Christ has died, Christ has risen, and Christ will come again.

This leads to the final point, which addresses the main reason that writers never start, get stuck, or give up: *fear*. All writers experience some level of fear about writing.[151] This is not only true of unpublished writers, but of popular and critically successful writers as well.[152] It might be a fear of failure. It might be that they will not meet their potential, or that their second book will not be as good as their first.[153] It might be what is popularly called "impostor syndrome." It's that sense that all your success is a fluke and soon the world will realize that they were wrong about you. Frederick Buechner, in an interview for *Of Faith and Fiction* said that, "What robs me of real gratification is what I think I inherit from my past, the feeling of 'if they only knew.'"[154]

---

[151] "I spend vastly more time nowadays trying to figure out what's stopping me from doing the work, trying to figure out how I can become the person who can do the work, investigating the shame and fear: the shame of self-exposure, the fear of ridicule or condemnation, the fear of causing pain or harm." Jonathan Franzen, "The Art of Fiction, No. 207," *The Paris Review*, No. 195 (Winter 2010) accessed October 16, 2013, http://www.theparisreview.org/interviews/6054/the-art-of-fiction-no-207-jonathan-franzen

[152] "I suffer as always from the fear of putting down the first line. It is amazing the terrors, the magics, the prayers, the straitening shyness that assail one. It is as though the words were not only indelible but that they spread out like dye in water and color everything around them. A strange and mystic business, writing. Almost no progress has taken place since it was invented. The Book of the Dead is as good and as highly developed as anything in the 20th century and much better than most. And yet in spite of this lack of a continuing excellence, hundreds of thousands of people are in my shoes—praying feverishly for relief from their word pangs." Steinbeck, "The Art of Fiction, No. 45".

[153] "...But the bad news is that if you're at all like me, you'll probably read over what you've written and spend the rest of the say obsessing, and praying that you do not die before you can completely rewrite or destroy what you have written, lest the eagerly waiting world learn how bad your first drafts are." Lamott, 8.

[154] W. Dale Brown, 41.

For our purposes, the source of the fear, or its particular vintage, is less important than the impact of the Lordship of Christ on that fear. Because Christ is the Sovereign (King) over all things, the Christian writer does not need to live in fear. 1 John 4:18 says that, "There is no fear in love. But perfect love drives out fear, because fear has to do with punishment. The one who fears is not made perfect in love." Likewise in 1 Timothy 1:7 we read that, "For the Spirit God gave us does not make us timid, but gives us power, love and self-discipline."

For the Christian writer this means that we can write without worrying about achieving some idealized perfection. And this is particularly important because striving for perfection is a temptation for many writers. However, Christians confess that their "perfection" comes, not through their own efforts, but through being adopted children of God. Romans 8:14-17 says,

> For those who are led by the Spirit of God are the children of God. The Spirit you received does not make you slaves, so that you live in fear again; rather, the Spirit you received brought about your adoption to sonship. And by him we cry, *"Abba,* Father." The Spirit himself testifies with our spirit that we are God's children. Now if we are children, then we are heirs—heirs of God and co-heirs with Christ, if indeed we share in his sufferings in order that we may also share in his glory.

Therefore, Christian writers do not need to worry about gaining the approval of readers, critics, or other writers. Of course, comparing yourself to other people is not unique to writing,[155] but the Lordship of Christ means that God

---

[155] Abandonment is a necessary task of the writer. As we grow in our art, our art changes, and we must move on. One of the most generous spirits in twentieth century literature was William Stafford. He said the writer's job is to abandon his or her work, to allow others to make judgment of its worth, and to go on to the next poem, the next story. All of us have habits of thought. Often for writers they include formulas of disbelief in our own gifts. If we cannot let go of the familiar old habits, we will not grow as artist. To grow as a writer, we must open our hearts, grow in our capacity to learn, and deepen our courage. There is an ancient promise: "You will

has given us all we need.[156] It is not our place to demand more just because someone else seems to have talent or success[157] or achieves either with greater ease.[158]

The further impact of the Lordship of Christ is that Christians can more easily write out of a place of empathy, which is helpful because empathy is essential to good writing. Larraine Herring writes that:

> A writer without empathy is cold, detached, and preachy. A writer without empathy doesn't explore the unanswerable questions, but rather sticks firmly to what is known, or what she thinks is known. A writer without empathy creates stickfigure characters who represent ideas or judgments rather than people. A writer without empathy cannot create a world where you, the reader, can understand the characters, even if you don't agree with their actions.[159]

Christians should write non-fiction that is balanced, nuanced, and gracious. They should write fiction that is full of sympathetic, complex, and redeemable characters.[160] Christians should write this way because they recognize

---

know the truth, and the truth will make you free." Even those truths that are painful will ultimately increase my wisdom, undergird my strength, make possible my art." Schneider, 5.

[156] Matthew 7:9-11 "Which of you, if your son asks for bread, will give him a stone? Or if he asks for a fish, will give him a snake? If you, then, though you are evil, know how to give good gifts to your children, how much more will your Father in heaven give good gifts to those who ask him!"

[157] Matthew 25:14-30

[158] Matthew 20:1-16

[159] Herring, 39.

[160] "I hesitate to say more for fiction is far better experienced than interpreted. And so it is with sacraments. To fully understand a symbol is to kill it. So the Holy Being continually finds new ways to proclaim itself to us, first and best of all in the symbols of Christ's life, then in Scripture, and finally in created things, whether they be the glories of nature or art or other human beings...The job of fiction writers is to fashion those symbols and give their readers the feeling that life has great significance, that something is going on here that matters. Writing will be a sacrament when it offers in its own way the formula for happiness of Pierre Teilhard de Chardin.

that, "while we were yet sinners, Christ died for us." Christians know they were loved before they are worthy of love. And maybe Christ's example applies to writing too. Sometimes we need to write before we are "good enough"—before we are worthy of being read. Luci Shaw sums up the centrality of Christ in the life of a Christian writer when she writes that,

> If the gospel is foundational, out of it will naturally flow an art that does not deny its foundations but assumes it. If it is a given, we do not need to be reminded of its existence at every point. If our lives are centered in God's reality, we can risk working out from the center in new directions, each of which may hold the excitement of a fresh adventure.[161]

So does anything different happen when a Christian sits down to write? Perhaps. Or perhaps not. Admittedly, a lot depends on the particular writer. And still, it is undeniable that a follower of Christ has at her disposal several structures, practices, and beliefs, that, while imperfect, can be a great aid to her development as a writer. And the writing process itself is definitely an act of faith—it draws on the same spiritual muscles as faith in Christ. It can teach us to trust and let go. We may even learn to free ourselves from self-censorship and self-constraint,[162] not so that we can embrace hedonism, but so that we can fall into the arms of a God who loves us. Brenda Ueland writes,

---

Which is: First, be. Second, love. Finally, worship. We may find it's possible that if we do just one of those things completely we may have done all three." Hansen, 12-13.

[161] Shaw, xiii.

[162] "We abandon any image we may have of ourselves - including any and all concepts we may hold of art, spirituality, or creativity. To think consciously that we are doing spiritual art is not that different from doing art from money or fame. Any time we perform an activity for an outcome, even if it's a very high, noble, or admirable end, we are not totally *in* that activity. That is the lesson we draw from watching a child disappear in play. To dive into the instrument, to dive into the craft of acting or playing, into the micromoment, into what it's like to move our finger over the instrument, to forget mind, forget body, forget why we are doing it and who is there, is the essence of craft and the essence of doing our work as art. To the extent that we thus empty ourselves we can be spiritual artist. Unconditional surrender comes when I fully realize - not in my

Gradually by writing you will learn more and more to be free, to say all you think: and at the same time you will learn never to lie to yourself, never to pretend and attitudinize. But only by writing and by long, patient, serious work will you find your true self. And why find it? Because it is, I think, your immortal soul and the life of the Spirit, and if we can only free it and respect it and not run it down, and let it move and work, it is the way to be happier and greater.[163]

This could be as true for writers of non-fiction as for fiction. But one of the goals of this work is to promote the genre of story as a preferable vehicle of theological discourse and it is not enough to say, "We're going to miss the boat if we don't get on the storytelling bandwagon!" For the question remains: why stories? After all, even if you believe that the wider culture is going through a storytelling revival, this may only recommend the form on pragmatic grounds. (Depending on your attitude toward "culture" it might not recommend stories at all!) This is why the following chapter unpacks stories from rhetorical, communal, relational, personal, developmental,[164] biblical, and theological perspectives.[165]

---

brain but in my bones - that what my life or art has handed me is bigger than my hands, bigger than any conscious understanding I can have of it, bigger than any capacity that is mine alone." Nachmanovitch, 146.

[163] Ueland, 111.

[164] Using Osmer's terminology, this will be an *interpretive* task.

[165] This task will be *normative,* answering the question, "What should be?"

Chapter Four:

Why the Church Should Care about Stories

I was raised by Christian parents and part of my upbringing included being taught about the Bible. This took place mainly through its stories: Adam & Eve, Noah's Ark, The Battle of Jericho, David and Goliath, Daniel in the Lion's Den, the Nativity, and the Crucifixion. Granted, I got the watered-down versions that were appropriate for Sunday school—and these sanitized forms did their best to compete with Aesop's fables or the preachier of the Bernstein Bears books. Still, it didn't take me long to figure out that the *actual* Bible was closer to the original Grimm Brother's fairy tales: full of murder and war, slain giants, trickery and betrayal, God plaguing men, men tricked by women, women turned to salt—and what remains the absolute best story for every thirteen year-old boy—left-handed Ehud losing his sword in the fat of Eglon. It was messy and it was great.

The New Testament was gentler than the Old Testament, but even here the stories had more sizzle than the sanitized moral principles I heard from pastors and Sunday school teachers. After all, there was John the Baptist's severed head on a silver platter, Peter cutting off the ear of the guard, Ananias and Sapphira lying and dying. I don't remember the first time someone explained what "stoning" was, but I remember it gave me bad dreams for a week.

The reason these stories stuck in my head wasn't because I had a penchant for the macabre, but because storytelling is a hallmark of scripture. Johann Baptist Metz writes,

Theology is above all concerned with direct experience expressed in narrative language. This is clear throughout Scripture, from the beginning, the story of creation, to the end, where a vision of the new heaven and the new earth is revealed. All this is disclosed in narrative.[166]

The Bible tells a story; even the poems, letters, and apocalyptic literature weave together in one over-arching narrative that tells the story of God's action in the world. Jesus himself participated in the storytelling tradition. We call them parables, but they were stories—contemporary, accessible, and multilayered stories. Eugene Petersen writes that,

> Storytellers are our most honored users of language. In every civilization and culture, the story teller holds the center. Story is the purest and most democratic use of the language: young mothers murmuring lullabies to their infants, country singers spinning ballads, young people telling ghost stories around a campfire and preachers telling the "old, old story" from a grand pulpit, poets and novelists and playwrights published and unpublished.[167]

As I've outlined in Chapter One, many Christians have moved away from Jesus' pedagogical example. Stories may show up in children's messages or occasionally as heavy-handed sermon illustrations, but stories are rarely serious contenders for legitimate theological discourse. How many novels are assigned in seminary classrooms? How many churches form a small group ministry based on reading Chinua Acheba? Even when stories are a part of Scripture itself, preachers often explain away their power. And like explaining a joke, doing so drains it of its punch. You can feel this in Jesus' own words in Matthew 13 after

---

[166] Johann Baptist Metz, "A Short Apology of Narrative," in *Why Narrative? Readings in Narrative Theology*, Stanley Hauerwas and L. Gregory Jones, ed. (Grand Rapids: William B. Eerdmans Publishing Company, 1989), 252.

[167] Luci Shaw and editor, *The Swiftly Tilting Worlds of Madeleine L'Engle* (Wheaton, IL: Shaw Books, 2000), 59.

the Parable of the Sower. When Jesus' disciples ask him to explain why he speaks in parables, he says, "Because the knowledge of the secrets of the kingdom of heaven have been given to you, but not to them. Whoever has will be given more, and they will have in abundance. Whoever does not have, even what they have will be taken from them. This is why I speak to them in parables: 'Though seeing, they do not see; though hearing, they do not hear or understand.'"[168]

The Christian publishing industry has been guilty of producing stories that do not "see" because they do not reflect life, but rather some idealized (and highly subjective) version of it. Christians sometimes grasp so desperately for certainty and stability that, like Esau, they trade their birthright—of living into the complex story of God's action in the world—for whatever theological litmus test allows them to remain unchallenged and unchanged. By making this trade, they have given up a tremendous amount of the power of the Gospel to change the world. Robert McAfee Brown writes in *Persuade Us to Rejoice* about the story Nathan tells David in 2 Samuel 12,

> [This] reveals to us the extraordinary extent to which *a story has power*. It is important to remember whenever we are tempted to think of stories as no more than pleasant diversion from the sterner aspects of life, things we read to children or indulge in ourselves only when we've gotten caught up on the high priority items…Such an attitude sells the story form short. It is never as innocent as it appears—as King David has special reason to discover. Not only on Nathan's lips, but on many other lips and pages as well, stories have a surprising ability to sneak past our defenses and force us to look at things in a new way. [169]

---

[168] Matthew 13:10-13

[169] Robert McAfee Brown, *Persuade Us to Rejoice: the Liberating Power of Fiction* (Louisville, KY: Westminster John Knox Press, 1992), 25-26.

So why then, do many Christians view stories and storytelling as vacuous at worst and merely illustrative at best?[170] Besides the reasons laid out in Chapter One, another reason is that people understand faith as the intellectual affirmation of a certain propositional statement. But faith that is only propositional can lead to marriage vows that feel like a legal agreement, baptism that rings of bank transaction, and communion that is affirmed with our head, but never touches our heart. Even my own ordination vows did not pledge fidelity to the great story of God's action in the world, but to the "Holy Scriptures of the Old and New Testaments and as expressed in the *Standards of the Reformed Church in America*."[171]

If Christians reclaim storytelling, and not only as illustrative of some abstract principle, but as one of the primary modes of talking about God, they will gain a wider vocabulary of faith—one that resonates with the human condition. To do this Christians may need to understand the advantages inherent in the story form, the power stories have over humanity, and the theological reasons why stories might be preferred to traditional non-fiction theology.

The Qualities of the Story Form

---

[170] "I cannot attest to what goes on in Jewish or Catholic minds on this matter, but I can report that there are still Protestants who experience a lingering sense of unease when they turn to fiction instead of "serious reading." McAfee Brown, 25.

[171] *Book of Church Order, Reformed Church in America*, 12.

What is a story? This seems like a simple question. After all, we've been hearing stories since childhood: nursery rhymes, fairy tales, picture books, stories around the dinner table, at family reunions, around the campfire, in school, with our friends, and between co-workers. We tell stories of what we did this weekend, on our summer vacation, or what happened when the boss called us into her office. We tell children stories about when they were born, what it was like when *we* were children, and stories about what life *might* be like when they grow up.

So it can seem unnecessary to define what is, or is not, a story. But if we attempt the task, we soon discover how difficult it is, and this difficulty somehow justifies doing it. Flannery O'Connor warns that,

> I find that most people know what a story is until they sit down to write one. Then they find themselves writing a sketch with an essay woven through it, or an essay with a sketch woven through it, or an editorial with a character in it, or a case history with a moral, or some other mongrel thing.[172]

Now, there is no single definition of what constitutes a story. John Truby, in *Anatomy of a Story* writes that good stories focus on *desire,* which is part of a mysterious "dramatic code, embedded in the human psyche…an artistic descripting of how a person can grow and evolve."[173] Over a hundred years before Georges Polti reduced stories to thirty-six possible situations, including

---

[172] Flannery O'Connor, *Mystery and Manners: Occasional Prose (Fsg Classics)* (NY: Farrar, Straus and Giroux, 1970).

[173] John Truby, *The Anatomy of Story: 22 Steps to Becoming a Master Storyteller.* (New York: Faber & Faber, 2008) 7.

"deliverance," "self-sacrifice for an ideal" and "murderous adultery."[174] In 2004 Christopher Booker narrowed this down to seven models in his book *The 7 Basic Plots*. Booker sees stories as the repeated patterns of human experiences that build meaning over time, the way a wave builds as it moves across the water.[175] Adam Gottschal offers an even simpler understanding in *The Storytelling Animal* when he writes how,

> Stories the world over are almost always about people (or personified animals) with problems. The people want something badly—to survive, to win the girl or the boy, to find a lost child. But big obstacles loom between the protagonists and what they want. Just about any story—comic, tragic, romantic—is about a protagonist's efforts to secure, usually at some cost, what he or she desires.
> Story = Character + Predicament + Attempted Extrication.[176]

Part of the confusion around answering "what is a story?" comes because people sometimes use the terms "narrative" and "story" interchangeably. And in many cases that is fine, but for the purposes of my argument we need some delineation. Narrative is *a scene-by-scene structure: an arch that moves from one point another*. It is similar to *plot*. A thing happens, which causes another thing to happen, then another, which leads to still another. There is a causal relationship between events, even if, to the reader, the only identifiable cause is that the writer of the story has placed the events in that sequence.

---

[174] Wikipedia contributors, "The Thirty-Six Dramatic Situations," *Wikipedia, The Free Encyclopedia,* https://en.wikipedia.org/w/index.php?title=The_Thirty-Six_Dramatic_Situations&oldid=704425712 (accessed February 15, 2016).

[175] Christopher Booker, *The Seven Basic Plots: Why We Tell Stories* (New York: Bloomsbury Academic, 2006).

[176] Gottschall, 52.

This sequence of events is recounted by a narrator. There are various kinds of narrators: they may be a character in the events, a character outside the events, equivalent to the author, or so hidden as to be imperceptible. In this way a narrative structure can be applied to many different forms: sermons, video games, poems, and classroom curriculum.

A *story* uses the narrative structure and fills it with setting, characters and dialogue, the progression of time, and a point of view: all of which congeal to shape the reader's experience and determine the story's meaning. This is how a story creates a rich, vibrant, and complex form of human communication. And it is why it is a suitable form to talk about something complex—like God's action in the world—that requires context, nuance, a sense of process, and a consideration of lived experience. As we gain a deeper understanding of the different parts of the story-form we will gain a deeper appreciation for what storytelling offers Christians who want to say something about God, the world, and our role in it.

Setting

It was a dark and stormy night. How many times has Snoopy sat on top of his doghouse in Shultz's *Peanuts* and typed these words? They are so cliché that we can predict what words follow: *Suddenly, a shot rang out!* And yet it shows us that action happens in a particular place (during a storm) and a specific time (at night). Action without context can last a few sentences, but if it continues, it leaves the reader confused and frustrated. We need to know the circumstances of events to determine their meaning. We need to know the context in order to know how to feel and think. After all, the same action can mean vastly different things depending on the place, time, the people involved, and the surrounding events.

Another way of making the same point is to say that no one person, theological tradition, or school of philosophy sits in a seat of pure objectivity. We are formed and shaped by our lineage, schooling, experiences, and privileges. We have bodies, relationships, and personal preferences that could be understood as lenses by which we see the world. But even the metaphor of a "lens" is insufficient, for it implies that there is a "pure" self to do the looking and a "pure" world that we can see. Instead, we must remember we are part of the world and the world is part of us.

To various extents, the recognition of this contextualization has catalyzed social movements like feminism, civil rights, liberation theology, womanist thought, LGBT inclusion, queer theology, revisionist historians, issues of white privilege, and even, in a general sense postmodernism.[177] Some people will fight to return to an imagined, nostalgic narrative of 10, 50 or 200 years ago, but it is becoming more understood that any dominant social narrative must to exclude voices from the margins in order to maintain its purity and identity.

Therefore, when someone presents an opinion on a social issue or a book of the Bible, we are right to ask, "Who are you? Not just as a professional, or a scholar, but as a person? How did you grow up? What formed your thinking? What experience do you have with this subject? What is your privilege? How has it shaped your opinions? How do you understand your own body and the bodies

---

[177] Writer bell hooks repeatedly in her work summarizes what each of these must overcome as "the neo-colonial white supremacist capitalist patriarchy."

of other people?" In other words, "What is *your* story?" If theologians refuse to engage with (and share) their personal stories, they risk ending up like Snoopy, typing on their doghouses and saying that shots are ringing out, but forgetting to say why, or where, or to what end—and sounding cliché.

Not only must Christians recognize the contextual influences that shape their beliefs, they must recognize that they may not have the full picture of a situation. Context can always be broader. Just as there are more books than can be read in a lifetime, so too are there more ways of being a human in the world than we can understand. Amos Niven Wilder encourages us, when facing a decision to pause and "…ask not only, 'Is that a true story?' but 'Is that the whole story?'"[178] He argues that the reason for this question is the human tendency to see what we already know and reinforce what we already believe. He says,

> What we take to be true to life may be very shallow and distorted. We may like a story or a history just because it is true to life as *we* see it, but that story or history may be far from telling the whole story. A story may be all the better precisely because it is *not* true to life as commonly recognized. Even if it is true to what we may see as "a deeper view of life," that view also may be conventional and that truth very partial.[179]

Since stories *demand* a context in order to be sensible, they are a wonderful form for anyone wanting to say something about life. They force us to ground our comments in lived reality rather than floating off into abstraction. Rolland N. Hein writes,

> [T]he novel presents an imaginative vision of life in order to tell higher truth. This is the compelling quality of the serious novelist's

---

[178] Wilder, Amos Niven, "Story and Story-World" *Interpretations* 37, no 4 (1983): 362.

[179] Wilder, 363.

vision: he has something true to say about life, but he can say it only by embodying it in an imaginative projection of life in an imagined real world. What the novelist says instructs, and that profoundly.[180]

What Hein is arguing is that, to a large extent, the *medium* is the *message*.[181] The form we use shapes what we are trying to communicate. A story includes setting, character, details, and multiple layers. By including them as part of our message it communicates that these things are essential and important. A propositional statement like, "Jesus is Lord" is both simple and palatable. There is poetry in its unpretentiousness. And yet, sometimes marketing or a mob mentality take over and people develop a tendency to *oversimplify* the complex in order to make it digestible to the largest number of people. This is why so many self-help books include in their titles things like "the 7 steps," "10 best," or "5 principles." And this is why stories are a corrective: they are both complex *and* palatable.

Because stories require context to make sense, and cannot, without violence, be reduced to a moral or principle, in this way they can act as a "check" on traditional theology.[182] Like a pilot logging hours in a flight-simulator, stories test our theories against reality. In the science lab we can dissect a frog and make judgments based on what we find: we see large hind legs and guess that it is a

---

[180] Rolland N. Hein, "A Biblical View of the Novel" in *The Christian Imagination: Essays on Literature and the Arts*, ed. Leland Ryken (Grand Rapids: Baker Book House, 1981), 257-258.

[181] The phrase "the medium is the message" first appeared in the 1964 book *Understanding Media: The Extensions of Man,* by Marshall McLuhan.

[182] "In this way the theatre acts as a brake on all tidy philosophies: it maintains the existential character of existence against all attempts to relativize it; it shows that this existential character is a part of the all-embracing reality itself." Hans Urs von Balthasar, *Theo-Drama: Theological Dramatic Theory*, vol. 1, *Prolegomena* (San Francisco: Ignatius Press, 1988), 20-21.

good jumper and swimmer. Similarly, in the seminary classroom the teachings of Jesus can be broken down to their constituent parts. But engaging with a story is like watching the frog in its natural habitat: we see it as it jumps, eats, breeds, and lives. Keith Oatley writes that "For complex matters we may know how each part works, but we may need something like a simulation to see how the parts fit together in combination."[183] Stories can do just that.

Character and Dialogue

Stories throw human experience into the ring with confessions, traditions, and theology. Stories are not a list of principles or platitudes. They are people in real situations. As in life, it does not matter what is *supposed* to happen in a story, what the right choice *should* have been. What matters in a story is truthfulness. Sometimes people's lives force them to make complicated and inherently imperfect choices. It is situational ethics at its most specific. It isn't just the external context that gives a story it's meaning, but it is also the interior life of the characters.

Stories allow for something that most theology books lack: a look at the thoughts and feelings of characters as they process the events of their lives. This aspect is found in books like Augustine's *Confessions* and more recently in J. Todd Billings' *Rejoicing in Lament*. By contrast, most traditional systematic theology is not so forthcoming about the context and character out of which the work blossoms. In this way stories can release Christians from seeking after a

---

[183] Keith Oatley, *Such Stuff as Dreams: the Psychology of Fiction* (Oxford: Wiley, 2011), 17.

platonic ideal of faith and instead return us to the biblical narrative of the Incarnation. Actual *people* matter more than abstract *ideas*. Hans Urs Von Balthasar said it this way:

> [People] learn to go beyond their own point of view and assimilate that of others; things that were initially unintelligible or simply dismissed reveal an inner meaning, or at least become accepted as "a valid point of view"; teachers learn from their pupils, fathers from their sons. *What* people know is no longer a mere commodity, it is fused with the knowing person, people "communicate", "share themselves".[184]

This is quite challenging. Writing systematic theology from an academic, intellectual point of view does requires hard work and personal discipline, but such endeavors are regularly marked by lofty principles, logical gymnastics, and it often wags a shaming finger at dissenting views. Stories are a check on all these. H. Richard Niebuhr, writes how,

> Metaphysical systems have not been able to maintain the intellectual life of our community and abstract systems of morality have not conveyed devotion and the power of obedience with their ideals and imperatives. Idealistic and realistic metaphysics, perfectionist and hedonistic ethics have been poor substitutes for the New Testament, and churches which feed on such nourishment seems subject to spiritual rickets.[185]

Stories create layers of meaning and complexity by including various characters and dialogue. They can include contradiction, nuance, and various sides of an argument. Too many Christians are trying to iron out the wrinkles; stories remind us that wrinkles are part of the fabric of life.

---

[184] Von Balthasar, 35.

[185] Hauerwas, 23.

Point of View

The messiness of stories does not mean that they don't have a message or a point of view. Storytellers may not be as didactic as preachers, but that is because the form groans under the weight of a forced agenda. A good story is not reducible to a summary statement, at least not without doing violence to the story itself. If someone asks, "What is the story about?" the right answer is, "Read the story." Writer Flannery O'Connor spoke of how,

> A story is a way to say something that can't be said any other way, and it takes every word in the story to say what the meaning is. You tell a story because a statement would be inadequate. When anybody asks what a story is about, the only proper thing is to tell him to read the story. The meaning of fiction is not abstract meaning but experienced meaning, and the purpose of making statements about the meaning of a story is only to help you to experience that meaning more fully.[186]

The meaning of a story is the *totality of the story*. Each detail is essential, each word builds to create a unique experience that cannot be had apart from engaging with the story itself. Support for this idea, comes not only from literary studies, but also from the theological subfield of Practical Theology. Practical Theology recognizes the irreducibility of reality and pushes toward something called "complexification." John Swinton and Harriet Mowatt, in their book *Practical Theology and Qualitative Research,* explain the term: "[t]o complexify something is to take that which at first glance appears normal and uncomplicated and through a process of critical reflection at various levels, realize that it is in

---

[186] O'Connor, 96.

fact complex and polyvalent."[187] The authors even make the connection between wrestling with the world's complexity and using stories to address this complexity. "Stories are not simply meaningless personal anecdotes; they are important sources of knowledge. This is a difficult thing for the modern mind to take on board."[188]

Any high school student who has failed an American literature exam because they only read the CliffsNotes for *Lord of the Flies* knows that there is a difference between the story and a summary of the story. Summary statements of some of the greatest works of literature are so far from the stories themselves that they are almost worthless. What is *The Hobbit* about? Who is Ahab and why is he hunting a white whale in *Moby Dick*? Is Hamlet a "good guy" or a "bad guy"? These questions do not have easy answers. They require us to dive deep into the story, hopefully alongside other people, perhaps even under the tutelage of an experienced teacher. And if we *do* develop a list of "5 things" it will only be a shorthand reminder of our wrestling, a souvenir of the journey, never to be confused with the trip itself.

However, this does not mean the death of traditional critical reflection. Both traditional theology and literary study are tools help readers focus on a particular element within the larger story. For example, a teacher (of either subject) might draw attention to a particular symbol, widen the literary context, or recall historical events surrounding the writing—all things a reader may have

---

[187] John Swinton and Harriet Mowatt, *Practical Theology and Qualitative Research* (London: SCM Press, 2006), 337 of 5297.

[188] Swinton and Mowatt, 790 of 5297.

overlooked—not to extract meaning, but to add a new level of appreciation. The problem occurs when this secondary act, meant to flavor the meal, becomes all we can taste.

The Path to Transformation

Since stories take place over time, they can include within them a path to transformation. In a good story, a character *changes* from the beginning of the book to the end. John Truby writes that, "Character change, also known as character arc, character development, or range of change, refers to the development of a character over the course of the story. It may be the most difficult but also the most important step in the entire writing process."[189]

Watching as characters learn, grow, and change not only makes a story interesting, but also offers readers a second-hand, but legitimate, opportunity to learn, grow, and change. Stephen Crites writes that, "Only narrative form can contain the tensions, the surprises, the disappointments and the reversals and achievements of actual, temporal experience."[190] This means that a good story will show the *results* of a transformation in the lives of a character[191] as well as a vision of the *path* to transformation for the reader.[192]

---

[189] Truby, 77-78.

[190] Stephen Crites, "The Narrative Quality of Experience", in *Why Narrative? Readings in Narrative Theology*, Stanley Hauerwas and L. Gregory Jones, ed. (Grand Rapids: William B. Eerdmans Publishing Company, 1989), 82.

[191] Not all stories contain positive transformations. "Cautionary tales" contain characters whose decisions we are not meant to be emulate. See: *Crime and Punishment*.

It is the very structure of stories themselves that leave space for, even *require*, growth, movement, inconsistency, and transformation. Even non-linear stories—stories told in reverse chronological order for example—are still encountered by the reader in a linear way. One chapter is read, and then the next, then the next, on and on until the end. This is true even if chapters move the reader around within "story time." In this way the reader moves and grows along with the characters. Because of their scene-by-scene structure, stories do more than present data to support one side of an argument, they *move a reader from one point to another*, often without a reader even being aware of what is happening. Stories affect people differently than other forms of literature, because, for a short time, readers turn over the control of their consciousness to an author and live along side the story's characters. And when they return to their own world and their own lives, they do not return unchanged.

The Power of the Story Form

The Rhetorical Benefits

---

[192] This is contrasted to some Christian authors who write about a specific topic, or with a specific agenda. There are plenty of books that can be reduced to "be a man of God," or "sex is only for marriage," or even, "believe and be saved." These books may be clear, biblical, and convincing, but too often, all they do is paint a picture of unattainable perfection. They do not contain within their structure a vision of the *process of transformation*. If a reader is only offered the entry point of unattainable perfection, it is unlikely they will be able to change their life.

Storytelling is a rhetorical powerhouse. If you want people to remember what you have to say, wrap it in a story. If you want to change people, tell them a tale.[193] Good stories grip us because they are simultaneously familiar and surprising. The familiarity makes us feel comforted while the surprise tickles our evolutionary mechanism for fight, flight, or freeze. The most engaging stories use this tension masterfully, leading us to a conclusion that seems both inventive and inevitable. This engagement makes stories *pleasurable* to us, which, on the level of brain chemistry, means we read fiction differently than nonfiction. Adam Gottschall in *The Storytelling Animal*, writes. "When we read nonfiction, we read with our shields up. We are critical and skeptical. But when we are absorbed in a story, we drop our intellectual guard. We are moved emotionally, and this seems to leave us defenseless."[194] Stories are able to get past our normally guarded postures. This alone may be enough to recommend stories to anyone trying to reach a world that may be hostile to their message, including the message of the Gospel of Jesus Christ.[195]

---

[193] "The emotions of fiction are highly contagious, and so are the ideas. As the psychologist Raymond Mar writes, "Researchers have repeatedly found that reader attitudes shift to become more congruent with the ideas expressed in [fiction] narrative." In fact, fiction seems to be more effective at changing beliefs than nonfiction, which is *designed* to persuade through argument and evidence." Gottschall, 150.

[194] Gottschall, 152.

[195] "Years ago I read a man named Machado de Assis who wrote a book called *Dom Casmurro*. Machado de Assis is a South American writer—black father, Portuguese mother—writing in 1865, say. I thought the book was very nice. Then I went back and read the book and said, Hmm. I didn't realize all that was in that book. Then I read it again, and again, and I came to the conclusion that what Machado de Assis had done for me was almost a trick: he had beckoned me onto the beach to watch a sunset. And I had watched the sunset with pleasure. When I turned around to come back in I found that the tide had come in over my head. That's when I decided to write. I would write so that the reader says, That's so nice. Oh boy, that's pretty. Let me read that again." George Plimpton, "Maya Angelou, the Art of Fiction No. 119," *The Paris Review*, Fall

The Personal Benefits

But stories aren't just useful in changing *other* people. They are useful in changing *ourselves*. Studies have shown various personal benefits of engaging with stories. James W. Pennebaker and Janel D. Seagel reported in the *Journal of Clinical Psychology* that, "The act of constructing stories is a natural human process that helps individuals to understand their experiences and themselves." They go on to outline how stories allow people to organize and remember their experiences while, "integrating thoughts and feelings." This gives people a "sense of predictability and control over their lives." Therefore, it might be possible for people to let go of troubling experiences and thought patterns via storytelling—a theory verified by psychologists and writing retreat leaders. Writing about our lives has been shown to result in fewer visits to the doctor for adults as well as better grades for students.[196]

We are each the protagonist in our own story. We both arrange the past to make meaning of the present and envision a future that we believe we are moving inevitably toward. According to Lawrence Palmiere Peers it is when reality breaks into these narratives that people are most likely to seek psychological help. It is, "when the narratives in which they are 'storying' their experience, and/or in which they are having their experience 'stories' by others, do not sufficiently

---

1990, 1, accessed August 28, 2015, http://www.theparisreview.org/interviews/2279/the-art-of-fiction-no-119-maya-angelou.

[196] James W. Pennebaker and Janel D. Seagal, "Forming a Story: The Health Benefits of Narrative," *Journal of Clinical Psychology*, Vol 55(10), (1999): 1243-1254.

represent their lived experience."[197] People either need to change their life to fit their story or their story to fit their life. This is especially true for victims of trauma, whose fracture between the story they had been telling themselves and their lived reality is so wide that they often have difficulty with day-to-day functioning.[198] Pennebaker writes how, "The beauty of a narrative is that it allows us to tie all of the changes in our life into a broad comprehensive story. That is, in the same story we can talk both about the cause of the event and it's many implications."[199]

The Evocation of Emotions

There are historic philosophical, religious, and psychological conversations *about* emotions, but these are usually intellectual exercises, they rarely *contain* or *evoke* emotions in the reader. Yet, to have a theological conversation that does not include something as fundamental as human emotion—and not merely as a referent, but as something directly experienced—seems to divide what it means to think from what it means to be human. It is like cooking without heat. We may stir ingredients in a pan and serve them to our guests, but nothing happens. There is no sizzle, smoke, or pop.

---

[197] Lawrence Palmieri Peers, "Recreating Congregational Stories: Insights from Narrative Therapy" *Congregations* 30, no 4 (fall 2005), 16.

[198] Susan Zimmermann, *Writing to Heal the Soul: Transforming Grief and Loss Through Writing* (New York: Three Rivers Press, 2002).

[199] Pennebaker, 1250.

This is because emotion is the fire on which we cook our ideas, principles, and theories. Of course, not all stories evoke all emotions in everyone,[200] but many of our best stories evoke happiness, love, pride, sadness, and anger. Stories can arouse us sexually, inspire us to change our lives, and linger in our minds long after we have put them down. This fact alone makes stories one of the more interesting forms available to anyone wanting to say something about the human condition.

But because stories contain both the "cause of an event and its many implications" it can contain both the ingredients for our meal and the heat for cooking them. It is a fully integrated tool for healing and transformation. The ingredients would be the point of view of a story—what it says about the way the world works. But the heat is the emotion a character feels while navigating the world. The combination of these is what makes storytelling an interesting tool, because, by providing just enough distance between a reader and a character, it can sometimes allow a reader to feel emotions that would otherwise be to too raw to handle face-on in their own lives.

Stories Build Empathy

When you read a story, you imagine yourself into the world of the story through a process called "transposition." The better the story, the more engaged the reader, and the greater level of transposition. If you've ever finished a really good book and looked around with a sense of disorientation, needing to remind

---

[200] "The capacity of a particular novel to invoke readers' empathy may change over time (and some texts may only activate the empathy of their first, immediate audience)." Suzanne Keen, *Empathy and the Novel*, (Oxford: Oxford University Press, 2007), 74.

yourself of where—or perhaps even *who*—you are, then you've experienced transposition.

It is the experience of transposition that gives stories the ability to increase empathy in readers. For example, I am a 36 year-old, American male. Because I live in a racialized world, I may not believe that I have anything in common with a 65 year-old, Tibetan grandmother. But if I read a story about her life—her joys, struggles, and particularities—and find a point of human connection, then that experience will transfer to my lived experience of other people. They next time I meet someone who I initially judge to be different, not only will I remember the story, but I will have a different emotional reaction. I will have a greater level of empathy. P. Matthijs Bal and Martijn Veltkamp looked into this exact question and found that,

> [T]here is evidence suggesting that seeing or reading about another person experiencing specific emotions and events activates the same neural structures as if one was experiencing them oneself, consequently influencing empathy.[201]

In *Empathy and the Novel,* Suzanne Keen writes that empathy is, "A spontaneous sharing of feelings, including physical sensations in the body, provoked by witnessing or hearing about another's condition."[202] Now, Keen is a

---

[201] Bal PM, Veltkamp M, "How Does Fiction Reading Influence Empathy? An Experimental Investigation on the Role of Emotional Transportation," PLoS ONE 8(1): e55341. Doi:10.1371/journal.pone.0055341.

[202] She continues, "Human beings and other primates frequently experience fleeting empathetic sensations, which can be observed and measured by physical signs, including facial expression, decreased heart rate, altered skin conductance, and palm sweat. These signs can be captured by observation and, in the lab, by electromyographic (EMG) recordings and even fMRI imagery of brain activity. These common experiences may go by too quickly to register in our long-term memory, but most people, when asked, can recall times when they felt *with* another (as opposed to feeling *for* another, or sympathy)." Suzanne Keen, *Empathy and the Novel* (Oxford: Oxford University Press, 2007), xxi.

guarded scholar and warns that the relationship between stories and empathy is not as clear as some proponents of story (like myself) would like.[203] But even she admits that, "The mass appeal of empathetic fiction may not translate directly into altruism, but its very success in the marketplace demands attention."[204]

The empathy-raising ability of stories comes, in part, from something called *mirror neurons*. "When we see someone smile, we tend to smile back. When we see someone frown we too tend to frown. Oatley writes, "We recognize emotion by activating our own comparable experience and expression of a similar emotion."[205] Scientists have put people in MRI machines and given them direct experiences of, for example, a sour-flavored drink, and then shown them pictures of other people drinking something sour and found that the brain activity registers the same thing. When we yawn after someone else yawns or when our eyes water when someone tells us they have something stuck in their eye, we testify to the role of mirror neurons. Gottschall interviewed a neuroscientist who said,

> Whether we see a movie or read a story, the same things happens: we activate our bodily representations of what it feels like…and that is why reading a book and viewing a movie can both make us feel as if we literally feel what the protagonist is going through.[206]

Part of empathy is remembering that there are thousands of ways of being a person and that most people are trying to do the best they can. By reading many,

---

[203] For example, many people overlook the potential *negative* affect of stories on people, or to a lesser degree, the trivial or consumer elements of stories being a product that is being sold by people who need to make money on the sale.

[204] Keen, 99.

[205] Oatley, 113.

[206] Gottschall, 62-63.

many stories we correct our tendency to be drawn to information that reinforces our own particular view of the world. The collected stories of humanity often present opposite, but equally valid perspectives. By reading stories by and about people we initially judge to be different from ourselves, we develop our capacity to live within complexity and tension. We may even begin to see ourselves as more complex, nuanced, and flawed. Thomas Howard, in *The Christian Imagination: Essays on Literature and the Arts* writes,

> By participating in the noble fictions of the human imagination, we enlarge our capacity to apprehend experience. There comes a sense both of the oneness of human experience and of its individuality…As a man becomes familiar with the follies, sins, and troubles of the great characters in fiction and drama—Tom Jones, Henry V, Jane Austen's Emma, George Eliot's Dorothea, Hardy's Tess, James's Isabel, Tolstoy's Anna—he realizes that here are profound probings by noble minds of the ambiguities of human experience, and his own appreciation of the ambiguities is sharpened.[207]

As we read stories, we broaden our understanding of the number of legitimate ways of being in the world. We are able to understand the "follies, sins, and trouble" of the human character. We are therefore less likely to reduce complex situations to incomplete (therefore inaccurate) but manageable summary statements. And we may also find ourselves more critical of our own narrative and the traditions in which our lives our rooted.[208]

---

[207] Thomas Howard, "Homer, Dante, and All That," in *The Christian Imagination: Essays on Literature and the Arts*, ed. Leland Ryken (Grand Rapids: Baker Book House, 1981), 129.

[208] "An advantage to readers whose common treasure is the common Book, and for whom common prayer and a common sense that salvation is both desirable and not a purely individual matter, is that they can become confident enough in their own identity to take the ultimate concerns of others, past and present, a little more seriously. They should be able—they have not entirely forgotten their calling—to give to our own older literature a comparably

Stories Build Community

Stories allow us to travel to places we could never see in ten lifetimes. We can go to lands that don't exist—have *never* existed! This is not escapism. People who get lost in storylands are not escapists. The "lonely librarian" is a trope. In fact, studies have shown that there is a correlation between people who read only *non*fiction and loneliness (and lower levels of social support).[209] It might be too much to claim that reading stories makes friends, but Anne Lamott writes how,

> I started writing a lot in high school: journals, impassioned antiwar pieces, parodies of the writers I loved. And I began to notice something important. The other kids always wanted me to tell them stories of what had happened, even—or especially—when they had been there. Parties that got away from us, blowups in the classroom or on the school yard, scenes involving their parents that we had witnessed—I could make the story happen. I could make it vivid and funny, and even exaggerate some of it so that the event became almost mythical, and the people involved seemed larger, and there was a sense of larger significance, of meaning.[210]

One reason people who value stories might be more socially connected is because stories build community. This is why my childhood introduction to the Bible was through stories and why stories have been used for generations to teach

---

responsible treatment of its primary religious and moral as well as stylistic dimensions." Jeffrey & Maillet, 324.

[209] "The stereotype of people who read a lot is that they are lonely and socially isolated. In this second study (the one in which we also measured personality) we looked into this question. We found that reading fiction was not associated with loneliness, but was associated with what psychologist call high social support, being in a circle of people whom participants saw a lot, and who were available to them practically and emotionally. Loneliness and low social support were, however, associated with reading predominantly non-fiction. Insofar, therefore, as the stereotype of readers being socially isolated is accurate, it applied more to non-fiction readers than to fiction readers." Oatley, 159-160.

[210] Lamott, xix.

young people the ways of their community.[211] And the telling of stories goes beyond passing evolutionary survival techniques from one person to another or from one generation to another. Stories bind people together.

For example: think of any group of people; it could be determined by geography, political affiliation, racial or national identity; it could be your family, school, or even the fans of your favorite sports team. Then think about the stories that get told and retold by members of this group. Whether it is the 'Christmas the basement flooded' or the sports team that is a perennial loser, or how America threw off British tyranny, stories bind people together. This is why, when my country wins an Olympic gold, I feel proud. I didn't have anything to do with the win, but my story has been interwoven with my country and it means that I get to share in the pride (or shame) when my country does something.[212]

Stories Cross Boundaries

---

[211] "Modern psychology is based on the therapist's recognition of the stories taught to us by our parents, teachers, clergy, and peers and of their effects on us. Out of this tapestry of history and values, we began, as children, to weave our own story, subconsciously accepting certain threads we'd inherited and rejecting others. Eventually the stories we swallowed and digested began living in us, governing our emotions and choices. They became the stage for enacting our beliefs. The more we identified with our stories, the more power they gained to shape our view of reality. With this power we subconsciously enroll everyone we encounter into believing our stories just as we do…The nature of the role in which we have cast ourselves is irrelevant. Regardless of whether we see ourselves as the good child, the happy wanderer, the loyal friend, the martyred parent, the hard worker, the heroic survivor, the perpetual victim, the die-hard rebel, the serious thinker, the devoted lover, the responsible citizen, or the free spirit, we have invested our role with tremendous power-the power to define us and guide us, the power to destroy us, and the power to heal us." Cerwinske, 15-16.

[212] "Story, in other words, continues to fulfill its ancient function of binding society by reinforcing a set of common values and strengthening the ties of common culture. Story enculturates the youth. It defines the people. It tells us what is laudable and what is contemptible. It subtly and constantly encourages us to be decent instead of decadent. Story is the grease and glue of society: by encouraging us to behave well, story reduce social friction while uniting people around common values." Gottschall, 137-138.

At the same time that stories build communities, they also push and cross boundaries. While stories can reinforce dominant social narratives, they can also challenge them. On a personal level, I have been changed by hearing the stories of friends and family on issues of fertility, sexuality, abortion, addiction, Alzheimer's, dying, cancer, the church, faith, and God. These stories may not always mesh with orthodox belief, but because of the power of stories and the love I feel for my friends, I cannot dismiss these stories even if I wanted to. And it isn't just the individual who is affected by stories; *social* change can also happen through stories.

This happens because when an issue becomes a lived reality, rather than an abstract talking point, it shifts the cultural understanding. This is currently happening around the issue of same-sex relationships. It's a narrative that's almost formulaic. First, a person believes homosexuality to be a sin. Next, they hear the story of someone who is gay, which moves it from an "issue" to a deeply complex story in which they are playing a role. Finally, their stance on the issue either becomes more nuanced or changes altogether. A too-short selection of books that have influenced social opinion in this way are *Uncle Tom's Cabin, The Grapes of Wrath, The Jungle, Native Son, Cry the Beloved Country, The Autobiography of Malcolm X, 1984, Brave New World, Silent Spring, Beloved, Things Fall Apart,* and *The Kite Runner.*[213]

---

[213] "[E]mpathetic fiction (much of it written by women, racial and ethnic minorities, and postcolonial citizens) reaches a wide readership. In celebrated cases this fiction transcends barriers of difference represented by race, nation, gender, sexual orientation, and religion, among others. Through the long-term political, social, and ethical consequences of empathetic reading experiences have yet to be demonstrated, the ardency of readers and the perseverance of novelists give pause to the skeptic who would argue that literature makes nothing happen." Keen, xxiv-xxv.

In this way, stories can be the vanguard of social acceptance.[214] Before

society embraces a change, a story must cross over a line of privilege and

power.[215] If we encourage people to tell their stories, those on the margins will

begin to challenge the dominant narrative.[216] Hearing the stories of other people

does not place us on the slippery slope of subjectivity. We will still be able to

make thoughtful judgments, but we will need to redefine how we make them. As

stories from the margin begin to test and shape the dominant narrative, Hans Urs

Von Balthasar reminds us that, "It is less a matter of weighing arguments than of

displaying how adopting different stories will lead us to become different sorts of

persons. The test of each story is the sort of person it shapes."[217] And if this isn't

---

[214] "As the linguist Noam Chomsky showed, all human languages share some basic
structural similarities - a universal grammar. So too, I argue, with story. No matter how far we
travel back into literary history, and no matter how deep we plunge into the jungles and badlands
of world folklore, we always find the same astonishing thing: *their stories are just like ours.* There
is a universal grammar in world fiction, a deep pattern of heroes confronting trouble and
struggling to overcome." Gottschall, 55-56.

[215] "The task before us was not to determine which version of the story was correct and
which wasn't. Instead it was to recognize that there were many competing stories the congregation
could tell. In this psychic and social space where multiple interpretations of the past were now
exposed, the task before us was not to determine whose version of the story was "true" but to
choose how to move forward." Peers, 18.

[216] "Revisionist historians such as Howard Zinn and James Loewen have argued that
American history texts have been whitewashed so thoroughly that they don't count as history
anymore. They represent determined forgetting - an erasure of what is shameful from our national
memory banks so that history can function as a unifying, patriotic myth...The myths tell us that
not only are we the good guys, but we are the smartest, boldest, best guys that ever were."
Gottschall, 124-125.

[217] Stanley Hauerwas and David Burrell, "From System to Story" in *Why Narrative?
Readings in Narrative Theology*, Stanley Hauerwas and L. Gregory Jones, ed. (Grand Rapids:
William B. Eerdmans Publishing Company, 1989), 185.

clear enough, he writes that, "Action on the world stage will always be determined in part by how the man in the lowly role is viewed."[218]

The Theology of the Story Form

But however strong the case for adopting stories on utilitarian or social grounds, there are deeply theological reasons for preferring stories to other forms. In the 1973 book *Theo-Drama,* Von Balthasar wrote that because God showed up not as a doctrine, or through silent contemplation, but in *action*, and that this tells us about God's character, will, and purpose.[219] Further, he argues that this recommends the story-form as a beneficial framework for talking *about* God's action in the world. He writes,

> [I]f there *is* such a thing as theo-drama…and if it is fundamentally the event of God becoming man and his action on the world's behalf, there must be dramatic ways (legitimately so) of presenting it, be they ever so indirect, risky, precarious and ambiguous. And such forms of presentation…must yield conclusions with regard to the nature of this same theo-drama."[220]

What Von Balthasar is arguing is that when we talk about God we do well to follow God's example and choose a narrative structure for our conversations.

---

[218] Von Balthasar, 257.

[219] "For God's revelation is not an object to be looked at: it is his action in and upon the world, and the world can only respond, and hence "understand", through action on *its* part." Von Balthasar, 15.

[220] Von Balthasar, 112.

God works in both the large-scale story of human history,[221] but also in specific stories and events. The most specific action being the Incarnation of Christ, which is not a proposition to be affirmed or denied,[222] but a person who was born in a specific place, lived during a particular time, died a real death, and actually rose again.

Christ himself taught in principles and precepts at times, like during the Sermon on the Mount, but he is most known for his use of parables to instruct and evoke.[223] There is emotion in the Prodigal Son. There is social complexity and subtlety in the Parable of the Good Samaritan. There is tangibility and specificity to the Parables of the Sower, the Lost Coin, and the Treasure Buried in a Field. Each is drained of their power if they are reduced to moral imperatives: honor your father, help people, there are different kinds of people, look for what you've lost, seek a treasure. As stories they stick to our insides like hearty food on a winter day.

Testifying to Christ's example, the early church carried on the work of Christ, which was not to advocate strict adherence to the law, with its principles

---

[221] "A long-standing perception of overarching unity - regarding this whole library as if it were a single book - arises from the way the biblical books build upon each other as they engage an unfolding sense of an ultimate authorial presence, working in and through the manifold histories and poems, shaping them toward a fullness of meaning that casts a light of understanding back over the collection as a whole." Jeffrey & Maillet, 111.

[222] The creeds and confessions are valuable affirmations, but they only have value if they point to a *real* person.

[223] "Interpretation of our meaning with the aid of a story is a well-known pedagogical device. So Lincoln told his homely tails and conveyed to others in trenchant fashion the ideas in his mind; so Plato employed myths to illustrate philosophy and to communicate visions of truth that ordinary language could not describe; so Jesus himself through parable tried to indicate what he meant by the phrase "kingdom of God." H. Richard Niebuhr, "The Story of Our Life," in *Why Narrative? Readings in Narrative Theology*, Stanley Hauerwas and L. Gregory Jones, ed. (Grand Rapids: William B. Eerdmans Publishing Company, 1989), 23.

and rules, but to tell and retell the *specific story of Christ*. H. Richard Neibuhr wrote that,

> The preaching of the early Christian church was not an argument for the existence of God nor an admonition to follow the dictates of some common human conscience, unhistorical and super-social in character. It was primarily a simple recital of the great events connected with the historical appearance of Jesus Christ and a confession of what had happened to the community of disciples. Whatever it was that the church meant to say, whatever was revealed or manifested to it, could be indicated only in connection with an historical person and events in the life of his community. The confession referred to history and was consciously made in history.[224]

The Church not only continued Christ's work, but by offering testimony to what they had seen and heard they used Christ's preferred method of instruction: storytelling. Was Christ was doing more than using an effective communication technique? If we assume that storytelling was a deliberate choice, not just a personal or cultural preference, we begin to see how Christ himself might have identified the structure by which salvation could be transmitted from generation to generation. For if the church continues to share the saving work of Christ, then there must be some element of the salvific itself event that is itself passed along in what Niebuhr calls this "simple recital."

This means that in the actual hearing of the story of Christ, listeners somehow participate in, or are interwoven with, the salvific act. Michael Root writes that, "[T]o speak of the redemptive significance of the story is to speak of the redemptive significance of a contemporary event, the telling of the story of

---

[224] Niebuhr, 21.

117

Jesus."[225] It may strike us as odd, but how else does the salvific act—which happened thousands of years ago—renew itself in each subsequent generation without some residue of the original event activated by the re-telling? The power of the story is a power of transformation. Robert McAfee Brown, writes that, "The power of a story is a power over which we do not have ultimate control, since it can catch us off guard, tell us things about ourselves we would prefer not to know, and liberate us to move in directions we would never have imagined."[226]

What is a Good Christian Story?

Where have we travelled so far? We have seen how stories are engaging, subversive, and transformative. They can bind people together and evoke deep emotions. They can cross boundaries and change cultures.

But this does not mean that all stories are equal. While there is disagreement, people regularly judge stories on their literary merits, not only by purchasing them, but also with awards, or by including them in classroom curriculum, or by inviting authors to conferences. These literary criteria should not be abandoned by Christians, but to them another layer must be added. Christians must also render a judgment about the quality of a story in terms of the

---

[225] Michael Root, "The Narrative Structure of Soteriology" in *Why Narrative? Readings in Narrative Theology*, Stanley Hauerwas and L. Gregory Jones, ed. (Grand Rapids: William B. Eerdmans Publishing Company, 1989), 265.

[226] McAfee Brown, 28-29.

direction it points us. Robert Paul Roth reminds us that, "Not all stories are good. Some stories are inadequate or misleading or deceiving. By their fruits you shall know them…The stories that are fully satisfying and edifying will prevail over the stories that are discriminatory and destructive."[227]

The question is then: From a Christian perspective, what makes a good story?

Alain de Botton is a humanist, but in his book *Art as Therapy,* he presents a vision of art that addresses the deepest needs of our humanity. And while he writes specifically about visual art, what he says applies to stories as well. He writes that in the ideal, "Artworks would look to commemorate, give hope, echo and dignify suffering, rebalance and guide, assist self-knowledge and communication, expand horizons and inspire appreciation."[228] This is a good list—one that Christians should affirm, but is insufficient because it has no relation to the story of God's action in the world.

Thomas C. Foster writes from an academic slant about how good stories resonanate with something intangible but historic:

> It's like this: something back in myth, something—a story
> component, let's call it—comes into being. It works so well, for
> one reason or another, that it catches on, hangs around, and keeps
> popping up in subsequent stories. That component could be
> anything: a quest, a form of sacrifice, flight, a plunge into water,
> whatever resonates and catch our imagination, setting off
> vibrations deep in our collective consciousness, calling to us,

[227] Robert Paul Roth, *The Theater of God: Story in Christian Doctrine* (Philadelphia: Fortress Press, 1985), 17.

[228] Alain de Botton and John Armstrong, *Art as Therapy* (London: Phaidon Press, 2013).

alarming us, inspiring us to dream or nightmare, making us want to hear it again. And again and again and again.[229]

But this too is insufficient for a Christian in the same way de Botton's list is: it lacks grounding in the Bible and theology. Foster seems to toss in the little phrase, "for one reason or another" but doesn't give a guess as to what some of those reasons might be.

Stanley Hauwerwas and David Burrell base their thoughts about these things on the Bible. They suggest that for a story to be called "Christian" it should display the "power to release us from destructive alternatives; ways of seeing through current distortions; room to keep us from having to resort to violence; a sense for the tragic: how meaning transcends power."[230] They add some nuance to their argument by adding that even if a story doesn't contain all these elements, that this should be how the story affects the reader.

But even while these criteria are based in Christian theology, there is still something unsatisfying about them. They stop short of offering a practical guide for evaluating stories, not only the stories we read in books, but also that are pitched to us in commercials, news programs, magazines, or by politicians and religious leaders. This is why I have developed the following questions. They are my attempt to dip my oar deep in the water and pull hard. These questions are subjective but not arbitrary; each assumes a view of human flourishing that is complex, communal, and changing. Answering them will not definitively answer

---

[229] Foster, Thomas C. *How to Read Literature Like a Professor: a Lively and Entertaining Guide to Reading between the Lines, Revised Edition.* Revised ed. (New York: Harper Perennial, 2014).

[230] Hauerwas, 186.

the question, *"Is this story Christian?"* But they create a framework to start to understand the shaping power of a particular story.

What does it contain and what does it condone? The Parable of the Prodigal Son contains broken relationships, fast living, licentiousness, and gluttony. This does not mean that the story condones these things. Christians sometimes (too often without reading them) condemn books because they contain sex, violence, sin, or taboo behavior. Not all stories contain characters we are meant to emulate. Most good stories are full of complex people, who are engaged in a mixture of good and bad behaviors. Instead, it is better to finish a book and ask, "What is the author trying to tell me about what this book contains?"

Does it help us see our own situation? The Parable of the Good Samaritan is an example of how a story can begin with it's hearers thinking that it's about other people, only to have the bottom drop out beneath them when they realize that it is, in fact, about the them. Similarly, good stories for a Christian will not merely reinforce the way we see the world, but will ask us to expand our worldview and ultimately change ourselves.

Are the characters and situations realistic? Matthew 12 begins, "At that time Jesus went through the grainfields on the Sabbath. His disciples were hungry and began to pick some heads of grain and eat them. When the Pharisees saw this, they said to him, "Look! Your disciples are doing what is unlawful on the Sabbath." Jesus responds the his accusers with a story about King David and his companions eating the consecrated bread. Jesus knows that hungry people need to eat and to deny them food for religious reasons ignores the reality of the situation.

When we read Christian books set in a quaint, rural town full of pastoral fields and family dinners, then we are reading *aspirational* fiction, which is a kind of escapism. A truly Christian story can entertain the deepest questions of humanity from a posture of openness and variety—even of changing one's mind!

Does the story leave a space for the tragic? And for justice? Jesus tells the story in Luke 14 of a young man preparing a great banquet who sends out invitations. People respond with various excuses: bought a field, bought an ox, and just got married. But the result is the same: I cannot come. So the young man orders that they bring in the destitute of the city: the poor, crippled, blind and lame. Jesus ends the story with the damning line, "I tell you, not one of those who were invited will get a taste of my banquet" (Luke 14:24). The Christian story does not wipe away the sin and the brokenness of the world—at least not yet. It looks fully at the pain—pain we cause one another and pain we bring upon ourselves—before providing a path forward.

Is there space for genuine choice? Stories present us with pictures of roads not taken and roads that might still be taken. Peter's denial and Christ's subsequent post-resurrection instructions to "feed my sheep" leaves plenty of unanswered "what if" questions. A good, Christian story will leave us open to legitimate alternatives we may not have ever considered. It will ask us to change what we think and how we act, but it will not demand it. It will offer us a choice. Jesus' own example often pulls the rug out from under his listeners—and us—by turning the question back upon itself. He does this masterfully in Luke 20 when some Pharisees are trying to trap him and ask him about paying taxes to Caesar.

Instead of engaging them on their terms, he reframes the debate by grabbing a coin and telling them to "give to Caesar what is Caesar's and to God what is God's."

Does the story offer us a path forward? Is there hope? Is there a warning? Does it present a way forward that allows us to avoid violence? Does the story point in a direction that is reflected in texts like the Good Samaritan, the Prodigal Son, and in Micah 6:8, "He has showed you, O man, what is good. And what does the Lord require of you? To act justly and to love mercy and to walk humbly with your God"?

This leads us to the final and perhaps most useful evaluative criteria: *what does it evoke in the reader?* Gratitude? Empathy? Self-righteousness? Smugness? Does it call us to deeper compassion for others and ourselves? Asking about the "shaping power" of a story will yield a subjective answer, but also a significant one. After all, a story truly exists only as the reader engages it. This means that different readers may have different reactions to the same story and therefore, this question yields the possibility that not all stories will be labeled "Christian" for all people. However, if more often than not, after reading a story, people find themselves aspiring toward love, joy, peace, patience, kindness, goodness, faithfulness, gentleness, or self-control, we are safe to say we have located something we can call a Christian story.

There are two criteria that are often applied to evaluating stories that should be ignored. These are 1) where it was sold and 2) if the author is a known Christian. Just because a book comes from a Christian bookstore, or it written by someone who professes to follow Christ, does not mean the work should be exempted from the criticism of the above questions.

Coming up with any criteria for judging stories as Christian is a messy task and one that I expect will need continuous revision. Part of the reasons for this is that the task my ultimately be impossible to achieve in a definitive way. There is something inherent to stories that is incredibly inefficient. It is easier to put people in boxes and label them with big meaningless words—words like conservative/liberal, white/black, Christian/non-Christian, than it is to see people as multi-faceted human beings who change and grow over time. Could a pastor realistically ask her congregation to read *The Brothers Karamazov* in order to discuss the problem of evil? How I dream of the day when it can be so, but for now, I don't think it would work. Beth Moore is simply a more palatable writer. And not everyone wants to have their world deepened and made more complex through engaging with stories. Living in tension and complexity is a sign of maturity and not everyone is interested in the hard work of growing up.[231] This, then, is the gift and the problem of embracing storytelling as a theological form: it will inevitably ask us to change the way we see God, the world, and ourselves.

---

[231] "Perhaps the chief value of a literary education grounded in the Bible as foundational text is the formation of an imagination wary of ostentatious reductionism of any kind." Jeffrey & Maillet, 330.

Chapter Five:

Conclusion

The trajectory of this work began on the springboard of the "storytelling renaissance" in American culture. Americans are engaging stories on a deeper level in both popular media and academic dialogues. From sports to psychology, from video games to politics, and from television to issues of racial privilege, story and storytelling are being rewoven into the fabric of our social conversations. Of course, people have always understood the world through stories, and to alter the metaphor slightly, storytelling is not really a thread to be selected (or not) as we design the fabric of our lives, but it is the loom on which we weave.

And yet, a certain group of Christians—mostly affluent, white, men—are not running eagerly to embrace this resurgence of storytelling. And while this is a generalization, as a generalization it raises questions about the American narrative that has dominated (and *dominated* is the right word) since the country's founding. The narrative of American exceptionalism has persisted for the above-mentioned group only because it excluded, often violently, those groups whose stories did not resonate with the belief that America was a country where anyone could, with only hard work and loyal citizenship, achieve safety, stability, and success. While voices of dissent have always been speaking, singing, and shouting, the Internet has increased the public deconstruction of American exceptionalism from many different angles, including race, gender, sexual identity, economic disparity, regionalism, disability, and intellectualism. In fact, even though some would claim otherwise, the narrative of American exceptionalism is weakening. We now live in a world where narratives compete, co-exist, over-lap, and intertwine. For a Christian in this context, to ignore, or worse deny, the validity of stories as legitimate forms of social discourse is to risk irrelevance in the former case and to commit an act of social barbarism in the latter.

Yet, before Christians can write, tell, and speak of stories, there were two questions that this work needed to attempt to answer. The first was: what is a good Christian writer? What are the habits, attitudes, beliefs, and practices of those people who are both Christians and writers? Are there things that are common to all or particular to some? This yielded a general picture of Christian writers as people who read, care about the craft of writing, embrace vulnerability with their whole selves, and who try to be hospitable—even pastoral—in their writing. Some writers even understand their work as part of the prophetic tradition of speaking truth to power.

The second question was related to the first: is there a Christian writing *process*? Could those characteristics identified in successful writers be formed and fostered in aspiring ones? What was different when a *Christian* sat down to write? The answer to these questions wove together the "best practices" of a writing pedagogy with traditional Christian disciplines like indwelling scripture, participating in church, and observing the Sabbath. There was significant resonance between these two areas that is was not hard to conclude that a

Christian writer, because of traditional disciplines, because of church communities, and because of the belief in the sovereignty of Christ, had a ready-made set of tools to help their writing practice.

Finally, we moved from focusing on writing to storytelling, making the case that the church should care about stories, not only for their utility, but also for psychological, social, and theological reasons. The argument went so far as to make the case that in the retelling of the story of Christ's salvific act, a residue of that original act was reactivated. We also laid out several suggestions for evaluating the stories we encounter as Christians: whether in books, movies, advertising, or politics.

But all of this has only paved the road I want to now drive down. I am going to use the story-form to justify the use of the story-form. The next chapter is a novella that addresses some fears and obstacles common to writers: temptations of familial duty, creative distraction, and public service. This novella is not supplemental or illustrative but hopefully the kind of storytelling we have been pointing toward: a well-told story full of rich theological themes. After all, if I believe the story-form can carry the weight of theologically complex themes like love, grace, transformation, and forgiveness, then I should be willing to use the form to describe what it means to write as a Christian. However, if this particular story fails, it will not be because the story-form is flawed, only that my ambition and vision have outstripped my skills as a writer and a storyteller.

Therefore, this project now moves from the general question of: "Can a novel communicate the truth of what it means to be a Christian writer?" To the personal question of: "Can *I* be the author of such a novel?" This places me in a position of great vulnerability—after all, I may fail in my attempt. Yet, by adopting a position of vulnerability I am also embodying an important element of what it means to be a Christian writer: to choose vulnerability instead of fear and trust that God has equipped me for this task.

Chapter Six:

Searching for E, a novella

1. Perfection

I finally had everything I needed. Yesterday I needed one thing, but today it was perfection. Today, I bought a mahogany letter-tray from Pier 1, which meant I finally had everything I needed. I took the letter tray out of its plastic shopping bag and carried it and my second cup of coffee, out of the kitchen, across the living room, and into my office.

I wanted to call it my "study," but I had spent 30 years at (the now defunct) Commodore Insurance, and I habitually called any room with a desk in it an office. I told myself that it didn't matter what I called it because, regardless of what I called the room it would be where I would finally have the time and space to write my novels.

When I placed the letter tray on the right-hand corner of my desk I felt the same satisfaction people must feel when they complete a complicated jigsaw puzzle. I never saw the appeal of jigsaw puzzles, not then, not now. Even so, I could see that there had never been a finer room in which to write. The wall opposite the door was floor-to-ceiling built-in bookshelves, custom made by Dale Flaneler, who I knew from church. Even with the discount he gave me, they still cost close to $3,000. The shelves were filled with books I had read, books I intended to read, and books I felt ashamed not to have read, even though I knew I probably never would. Several shelves were dedicated to how to craft a novel, construct a plot, find inspiration, and then find an agent. The only books that were out of place were the half-dozen books that people had given me after Evelyn died: books on grief, and why these things happen, and God's sweet consolation.

Gag me.

The desk was ample in both size and beauty, but did not overwhelm. It had been stained cherry, but Dale sanded it down when he did the shelves and used the same deep brown stain on both. I would have had him do the same with the filing cabinet in the corner if it was not steel. Instead I put a fern on top of it. The filing cabinet was empty except for the bottom drawer, which held important personal paperwork like insurance policies, appliance warrantees, and copies of my will. My vision was that I would soon fill the upper drawers with drafts and brainstorms and half-baked ideas and portfolio clippings.

The jewel of the room—my Excalibur, my Mjolnir, my one ring to rule them all—was a Royal Futura 800 typewriter. It was an eye-grabbing deep-sea blue and sat in the place of privilege on the desk. I would soon select a blank page from the full ream on the left side of the desk and then *tap-tap-tap-ding-zerrrrch-tap-tap-tap-ding-zerrrch.* I would pull sheet after crisp sheet of glorious prose out of the carriage and place them—eventually without even looking—into the letter-tray that I had, only moments ago, placed on the right-hand corner of the desk.

Kate had wanted me to get a computer. The last time I visited her, she had shown me the one she bought for her kids, but it took so long to turn on and I couldn't imagine waiting that long to get an idea down. All the cords and cables reminded me of someone on life-support, something the giant monitor did nothing to dismiss. In comparison, my Futura 800 was compact, independent, and complete unto itself.

I rested my hands on the keys, feelings the little bumps on the f and j keys. These little bumps held so much potential. I drank more coffee and looked out at a perfect morning. Since 1982, fifteen years now, Green Lake had been our summer retreat. Every June and July, Evelyn and the girls spent days and night here while I made trips into the office as infrequently as possible. The lake was big enough for water skiing, but small enough that you could make out who was pulling the boat and wave as they went past. Even now, in September, once the sun was up the lake would fill with noisy families. As I watched, the sun began to cut beams through the trees, slicing up the fog and the memories.

I had sold the house and moved here three weeks after the funeral. The house had sold more quickly than I expected, but since Evelyn and I had always planned on moving out here once I retired, it didn't feel too fast. I didn't think too much about the house. Ev had loved this place, always been alive and relaxed here. If I were going to be able to find her anywhere, it would be here.

She had died four months before her life insurance policy was set to expire, so while it was never my plan to make the move alone, it was some consolation that I could do it six years before we had planned. I was fifty-nine. I had time, money, and space in which to write. I had everything I needed.

But first I needed to warm up my coffee.

Back in my office I sat up straight, shook my neck, rubbed my arms, and flexed my hands, popping several knuckles.

Now, what was my story going to be about?

I stood up and began to pace the room like an apprentice lion-tamer.

I needed something. Anything. Something to get my fingers in the groove. A warm-up that I could throw away. So, without thinking too much about it, I typed the greatest first sentence of all time:

In th b ginning, God cr at d th h av ns and th   arth.

I stared at what I had written—what I had tried to write. I hit the return key several times and typed:

This is a t st s nt nc . Is my typ writer working?

Then, for no other reason than some rooted belief in the phrase, "Third time's a charm." I typed:

v lyn, why did you hav to go?

I then pressed the e key several times in succession, which advanced the carriage but left no mark on the paper. I peered into the beast's mechanical belly, but it was too dark, so I pressed the Royal Typewriter Co. logo, which doubled as the hood release. I inspected the beautiful gears and precise arms and lingerie ribbons, understanding little of what I saw. I pressed the e key again with the same non-result. I watched the fan of metal arms. There! There! There! Like a missing tooth there was a gap in the orderly rows. This time when I pressed the e I could see a stubby little pinkie-finger stand at attention, looking lonely and suspicious, like a dog that's done wrong.

I swept my eyes across the desk, but it was as perfect as it has been three minutes ago. I lifted the entire contraption, but there was nothing hiding underneath. I turned it over and shook it like a piggybank I didn't want to break. There were the usual rattles and clinks, but no sound out of place. I righted the box, and the lid, which I had not secured, slammed on my finger. I let out three surprisingly specific profanities as I sucked on my knuckle skin. I dropped to my knees so I could brush the carpet, believing it was possible that the key had been broken by its own momentum and flung onto the floor. If I was unable to see it, then maybe I could feel it. How far could it have gone? I felt angry with myself for having no memory of the event. As I tried (unsuccessfully) not to knuckle-bleed on the carpet, I had a hazy memory of writing Esther last week. Or was it Maggie? I found a penny, a paperclip, a pen cap, and a piece of string.

I stood and scowled at the room.

I set my glasses on the desk and rubbed the bridge of my nose.

Then I heard what sounded like the popping of a campfire, but it came from the deep under-sea caves of my brain, building physicality and sending sensation across my skin. I thought that if this was what a stroke felt like, it wasn't that bad. When my fingers began to tingle I guessed it was really a heart attack. But then my hands began to move independently of my mind. And decided not to fight them because it felt better not to and I was curious what they were going to do.

The middle finger on my left hand gently tipped a book off the top shelf and let it flop to the floor. Then, just as slowly, the finger next to it pulled the book next to that one. Then I began playing arpeggios up and down the shelves. I plucked Bach, before pounding out Beethoven, then ending with a modern, atonal piece that was all sweeping armfuls, despondent wails, and tears. The e key had to be here. However unlikely it might have flipped behind a book, I had to know for sure.

Yes! I remembered I had typed a letter. To Kate! To Kate! Ha! It was about something. Tuesday. It had been Tuesday because I had to…what had I done on Tuesday? It didn't matter, but I knew it was Tuesday. I ran to the kitchen to look at the calendar there. Today was Friday. Was I angry on Tuesday? What had I typed to Kate that made me angry enough to break the machine? No. I hadn't broken it. I had *not* broken it. It was broken but I definitely had not broken it.

The shelves were empty so I turned to the desk. I pumped the drawers like furnace bellows, which somehow worked to heat the room because I when removed my shirt it was wet with sweat. Each drawer vomited pencils, tape, note pads, glue, and office detritus. I left it wherever it fell. I pushed the typewriter around on the desk, almost knocking it off several times. I sumo-wrestled my filing cabinet away from the wall. I dug my fingers into the soil of the plant before taking it outside to dump it on the driveway. I kicked over a wastebasket. Then I did it all again: the books, the desk, the files. The floor was covered with everything except what I wanted.

I pressed the palms of my hands into my eyes and clenched my teeth until my jaw shook. I turned circles in the middle of the room. Then I saw the stack of clean, white paper. It was the one thing I had not yet touched. As I watched it, it began to pulse—a pulse I felt in my own chest, as if a superior heartbeat was overtaking my inferior one. I looked down at myself and saw the impossible. My chest cracked like a flower peeling open and spit out what appeared to be a large, speckled egg.

I tried to catch the egg and keep it from breaking—I instinctively knew its fragility—but I only succeeded in knocking it sideways into my desk. The egg cracked once as it hit, then again as it hit the floor. I clutched at my stomach with nausea and saw that my chest had closed, leaving a patch of white chest hairs that once been mostly dark. The egg rocked, cracked, and dissolved into dust. And then there stood in my office a small bird. It wasn't a baby bird, helpless and bare, rather a fully-grown adult bird whose species I could not place. I had never seen a bird that color before—the same red that Evelyn's fingers became after pitting cherries—a red so deep it was almost to black.

This creature, beautiful and terrible, looked me right in the eye, took a hop, then another, and a third, then flew out the open window. I ran outside but I could only watch as it flew over the water and disappeared into the trees on the far side of the lake. I could barely believe what had just happened, but in that moment I did not feel either sadness or surprise. I knew where the bird was going.

And I knew I was going to follow it.

Kate's neighborhood looked as if all the houses were pulled out of the hat of the three-trick magician. Each lawn was aggressively green, sustained by a cocktail of chemicals and community ordinances. As I crept along the street, searching for a house number I could not remember, the whole place felt to me like the corporate version of what a neighborhood was supposed to be. Was it 206? For some reason I had 206 Hickory in my head as their address, but the streets were an arboretum of social engineering: Sycamore, Evergreen, Oakes, and Maple. After a while, I begin to doubt my memory.

I had checked the number before I left, but I had not taken my address book along. Parked next to where 206 Hickory would have been if the house number had existed, I realized that I had not taken very much for a cross-country trip. I had a duffle bag on the seat next to me containing a handful of underwear and socks, an extra pair of pants, various shirts, and a copy of *If You Want to Write*, by Brenda Ueland. I had my wallet in my pants and my checkbook in my coat. I had forgotten a toothbrush, deodorant, and my shaving kit. I had a grand vision of traveling light, on the move, jumping from place to place with ease. Now, as I rolled down the window to let in some fresh air, I realized I could do all these things and also have clean teeth.

Should I just turn around and go home? This trip didn't really make sense. Kate would never even know I was here. I should at least be better prepared. I decided to find the nearest Walgreens when a white Suburban pulled into a driveway across the street—209 Hickory!—and two blurs shot out: my two grandsons. The boys tumbled and rolled in the grass, seemingly picking up whatever game they had been playing before school. They were followed by the shrieks someone not wanting to be left out of the fun. Little Kristen was still buckled in her space shuttle car seat and Kate appeared as a silhouette reaching backwards to unlatch her daughter. Kristin slid out of the vehicle and to the ground and scuttled off to join her brothers.

It was only then that Kate appeared to me. I have always known she looked like her mother, but at that exact moment, having not seen either of them in eight months, I couldn't have told you who was standing across the street. Kate was thirty-two. I met Ev when she was twenty-four. Time was a slippery thing. Kate scowled across at this stranger watching her children with an expression that was all Kate, breaking the spell that my own memory had cast upon me.

I got out of the car.

"Grandpa!"

"Dad?"

"Hey!"

I passed out hugs and dollar bills to the boys and picked up Kristen, who was only four and still loved to be carried places.

Kate kissed my cheek, "What are you doing here? I mean, I'm glad to see you, but I didn't know you were coming. I just picked up the kids from school. The house isn't clean. Is everything all right?"

I assured her that everything was fine, but she still seemed skeptical. I watched children fly around the weedless lawn. "Is was kind of last minute thing. Impulsive. I hope it's not a problem."

"No. No. I was just picking up the kids from school. Have you been waiting long? Are you going to stay for supper? Kids! Don't leave your backpacks in the middle of the driveway." She said. Even as she swept them up herself.

"Let's go inside."

I carried Kristen, who had grown since the funeral. Why hadn't I visited before now? What had I done all summer? Had they come out to the lake and I wasn't remembering it? The day of the funeral Kristen had insisted that I carry her, insisted to the point of tears. This made it difficult to talk to people and impossible to shake hands, but it was also extremely comforting. She would rub my neck and play with my ears as people told me how sorry they were for my loss. Her four-year-oldness made her impenetrable to my grief and I loved her for it.

When we got inside Kate began what was obviously a very practiced deconstruction of backpacks: removing half-finished lunches, random socks, and crumpled papers. "Sorry about the mess. You know kids." I looked around at the kitchen that could have been lifted out of *Better Homes and Gardens*.

"They send all these papers home. Most of them are nothing, just one of thousands of drawings or craft projects, but of course you have to look careful through them all because inevitably there will be one that includes critical information about an outbreak of lice, or a form that needs to be turned in, or an upcoming event."

I once saw an experienced poker dealer in Las Vegas. That man had nothing on Kate with her unzipped backpacks over the open trash can.

Without looking up she said, "Really, Dad is everything ok?"

Kristen was getting bored in my arms so she wiggled down and went to find her brothers. "Sure," I said, "Everything is good. Sort of."

Kate paused, her fist a rainbow of papers, "Sort of?"

"I mean there's nothing wrong. I'm not sick, the house hasn't burned down, church is going fine. I'm great."

"Why don't you just tell me what is going on? I can tell that something is going on and we can either dance around it or you can tell me." Kate hung the backpacks on the hooks by the door.

"Ok, I will. So you know that I have been setting up my study—my office—and that I wanted to write." She nodded and I went on, "So everything was all set."

Kate held up a finger and turned her head up the stairs, "DO YOU GUYS WANT A SNACK?"

Three kids gave a jumbled reply that I could not understand, but seemed to be clear to Kate. "HOW ABOUT POPCORN?"

Another loud but indiscernible response.

Kate grabbed a bag of microwave popcorn and got it going. "Sorry, you were saying."

I sat on one of the stools, "I was saying that my typewriter broke. It was the strangest thing too. I started typing and everything was working fine except that the e key wasn't working. The words came out on the page but…"

"Dad, this is why you need a computer."

"There's more that can go wrong with a computer. Anyway, the ribbons are good and the carriage is sound. It's a perfect machine except for this one thing. If I had the right piece I could probably fix it myself. But here's the thing: I can't find the missing piece. I can't find the arm that hits the page and makes the e. I've looked everywhere but it's just gone. I'm actually entertaining the idea that someone broke it on purpose."

Kate rolled her eyes, "No one broke your typewriter. I'm sure the piece is somewhere in your office and if you would look again you would find it. That's how lost things are. You look and look and don't find it. Someone else comes in and sees in in plain sight."

An image of my office appeared in my mind. "I'm fairly sure I looked as thoroughly as anyone can look. It's not in there. If it were an x or a z I could see just making the best of it. But it's an e and e is in everything."

Kate poured popcorn into three bowls, "So besides someone sneaking into your house and breaking your outdated machinery, what do you think could have happened?"

I scratched at my cheek and felt stubble, "That's the thing. It's a new machine. Mom got it about a year ago. It shouldn't have just broken like that."

"Did she get the warrantee? You know mom always liked the extended warrantee."

I could see the blue edged warrantee card. "No, I don't think she did."

"Ok, whatever. It doesn't matter. What I don't understand is what you're doing here."

"I've decided to drive to the factory and get a new part."

"Oh! Is it here in Lansing?"

"It's in…New York, so I figured I would stop by and see you, then Maggie, then Esther and make a road trip of the whole thing."

"Why don't you just call the company? I'm sure they would send you the part. We want you to visit, but then we could plan out what we would do. Remember how you're supposed to be retired now: early bird specials, walking tours, growing roses, stuff like that."

"Growing roses?"

"Or whatever else is your equivalent of growing roses. My point is that there are easier ways to do what you're trying to do."

I didn't say anything for a little while, "I'm not sure there are."

Our conversation was interrupted by the children, who came into the room like a runaway train on hardwood floors, sliding and slamming into walls and chairs.

Kate set down the popcorn, "Dad, we need to talk more about this."

"Maybe. But right now I've got to eat popcorn." I snatched a piece from Kristen's bowl and she giggled and crawled onto my lap.

Kate's husband Martin came home and we all ate dinner together. The tacos were spicier that I would have made them, but it was so nice to witness the normal, family routine of dinnertime conversation: how was school, pass the beans, *Oh!* wipe the milk, sit on your chair, you've got salsa on your chin. It soothed me in ways I could not have explained.

I insisted on washing the dishes. I told them how it was nice to have enough plates and bowls to make it worth running the hot water. I did not tell them that I had gotten in the habit of letting my own dishes pile up in the sink. It seemed tragic to run the water hot for only a plate or two. I couldn't remember the last time I'd run my dishwasher. No one tells you that these are the things that are going to be the hardest to deal with when you're living on your own.

After supper Martin told the kids it was time for bed and the boys moaned and groaned while Kristen hid under a blanket. But soon they were all laughing as he chased them around the living room and up the stairs. Kate joined me in the kitchen, drying dishes, and we talked about their lives: Martin was being recruited for an administrative position but wasn't sure he wanted to leave radiology. There was a rumor that an IKEA was going to be built thirty minutes west. A new family had moved into the neighborhood whose kids matched up well to their own, but they seemed a little wild and rowdy. I listened and nodded and smiled. I had forgotten the sweetness of life together.

A few minutes later the boys thundered back down the stairs, leaping the last few steps, Kristen trailing behind, holding to the railing and taking one step at a time. I was peppered with a hurricane of hugs and kisses and pokes and tickles, but Kristen wrapped her arms around my neck and refused to let go.

"You do bed." she said.

So I carried her up to her bed and tucked her in. Then she proceeded to tell me a story about someone named "Elft," who I could not figure out if references a real or imaginary person. Truthfully, I didn't care. That girl could have talked nonsense forever and I would have sat there. It was only as she started to rub her eyes that I dimmed the light.

"Grandpa?"

"What is it sweetie?" I said from the doorway.

"I saw a pretty bird today. A red bird. It was pretty."

"That's great honey." I suddenly had a hard time swallowing, "I'll make sure your dad kisses you goodnight."

"Ok."

"Goodnight."

I went to my room and took a shower. I was getting tired, but I put my clothes back on afterward and went downstairs. Kate and Martin had opened a bottle of wine and were sitting in the living room. They offered me a glass and I accepted.

"So Kate tells me you're taking a road trip," Martin began.

"That's right." I looked at Kate.

"And that it's all to fix a typewriter."

I nodded.

Kate jumped in, "We don't think you should go. It's one thing to come here, because we've got plenty of room and the kids obviously love having you around, but Maggie and Esther? Will they even have a place for you to sleep? Are you going to call them and tell them you're coming? Here we have a guest room that it always ready for you. In fact, we hadn't planned on talking to you about this quite yet, but Martin and I had been discussing whether it would be a good move for you to come to Lansing. You could even move in with us, if that's what you wanted. We could even add on a room if you needed more space than the guest room—a study all your own where you could escape the kids when they get crazy and do your writing."

I suppose I should have been surprised by this idea, but I wasn't. I knew she was making a lot of sense. My own father's last years were a real struggle and I promised myself that I wouldn't put my kids through the same fights over housing, and driving and taking medications that I had gone through. If she has asked I could have outlined the advantages myself, but Kate continued to talk.

"We could help you with things like fixing your typewriter. You wouldn't have to worry about mowing a lawn or shoveling snow. You could do what you wanted, but if you didn't feel like cooking you could eat with us. You don't need to respond now, but just think about it. And stay with us at least through tomorrow. We want to show you Lansing. We want to take you to our church."

"It's Saturday." I said.

"Our church has a Saturday night service we go to whenever Martin has to work on Sunday."

"Oh." I thought for a moment, "Ok. I can stay another day."

Martin put down his wine glass, "Now, actually, I'm not as opposed to this trip as Kate is." Kate frowned at her husband. "You're a grown man capable of making his own decisions. But unrelated, I do think it's not a bad idea to consider moving here. If not today or this year, then before ten years have gone by. When my mother died my dad withdrew from a lot of things and he went downhill pretty quickly. Not saying that's going to happen to you—only that I hope you are thinking through all the angles."

Everything they said made sense. And I did love being grandpa. It was a role that felt good in a hundred different ways. "I'll think about it. And I'm not just saying that. I really will think about it. And I'll stay around tomorrow for church. You can show me your city." That seemed to satisfy them. Perhaps it was the wine, but I had a bad taste in my mouth so I excused myself to bed.

In my room I found that Kristen must have snuck out of bed because there was a drawing of a bird on my pillow. A red bird. I could see her child's intensity, purpose, and energy in the lines of the crayon. I looked at the page for a long time. I set the drawing on the nightstand, dug out my copy of *If You Want to Write* and found my place,

> Religious men used to go into the wilderness and impose silence
> on themselves, but it was so that they would talk to God and
> nobody else. But they expressed something: that is to say they had
> thoughts welling up in them and the thoughts went out to someone,
> whether silently or aloud.

I began thinking again about what Kate and Martin had said about moving in with them. I was tempted. It would be so easy to just submit to them. I deserved a break didn't I? And I would be happy in living out whatever years I had left close to people I loved. And Maggie and Esther lived in big cities and had no children for me to be grandpa to. I shook my head and returned to my book. I read another page and came to this passage

> For when you come to think of it, the only way to love a person is
> not, as the stereotyped Christian notion is, to coddle them and
> bring them soup when they are sick, but by listening to them and
> seeing and believing in the god, in the poet, in them. For by doing
> this, you keep the god and the poet alive and make it flourish.

There was a *bang,* as if someone had thrown a tennis ball against the window of my room. I went to the window and looked out. There, on the ground was the red bird. I knew it was the one I had been following, knew it like I knew my face in the mirror. I watched it lay there, dazed from the impact with the window. There was as light knock on my door.

"Dad?" It was Kate.

I turned from the window.

"I heard a thud and wanted to make sure you're all right."

I pointed, "A bird. It hit the window." Kate seemed relieved.

"Yeah, they do that from time to time, especially around this time of year. I guess we're in a migratory route."

She wished me a good night and left.

I turned back to the window but the bird was gone.

I got into bed and took Kristen's drawing, flipped it over, and fished a pencil out of my bag.

I am so tired. There should be more words for tired. I remember reading that Eskimos of a hundred words for snow. There should be at least that many for being tired. One could be the tired of carrying rolls of sod for your father all summer. Another could be the tired of wanting something for so long then realizing you're never going to get it. There should be a specific word for that tired feeling that says that maybe dying wouldn't be the worst thing. Or maybe tired is like a casserole: the same ingredients, just mixed up together before being baked.

Maybe Kate's right. Maybe I should just stay here a couple of days. I will be all by myself when I get back home. Not that I mind being along, but I know it can go downhill. What if I did move here? I could just as easily write here as I could there, right? Ev would know what to do.

I woke up several hours later with the pencil still in my hand, the light on, and with a desperate need to pee. I went to the bathroom, came back to bed, and slept soundly until morning.

I woke with the sun shining in the windows. The clock said 8:45. Beneath the covers I stretched my legs but didn't get up. I turned over and saw an eyeball peeking through the cracked door.

"Good morning." I said. And the eyeball, as well that the rest of the little girl crawled up into bed with me. Her feet were freezing cold, but she snuggled down and lay still. However, peace was short-lived as her brothers rampaged in minutes later and began wrestling and tickling, until we were called for breakfast. I shooed them out the door so I could dress. Then I followed my nose downstairs to a table laden with pancakes, sausage, and scrambled eggs. I started with coffee but did a fair amount of damage on the food, more than I needed, but all that I wanted.

Around mid-morning we all piled into Kate's Suburban and drove around Lansing. We drove through MSU and they pointed out the Wharton Center, Spartan Stadium, and the Breslin Center. They took me to the kids' school, where each kid needed to show me their favorite part of the playground.

Then we drove north for about twenty minutes to an orchard and went apple picking. I had never been apple picking before, so as Martin and Kate began to fill their bushel baskets, the boys climbed the trees, and Kristen poked fallen apples with a stick, I just stood there watching, feeling out of place.

"Come on, Dad. It's easy."

"You just rip them off the tree?" I asked.

"It helps if you give it a twist while you pull. Here, watch." Kate pulled and twisted, then after a pause, the branch jumped back into place and Kate was holding a beautiful apple. "You'll get the hang of it. It's really no big deal. Here, you can start with this one." She held out the apple and I took it.

Martin piped up from the other side of the tree, "And it's ok to eat while you work." As if to illustrate he held up his own half-finished apple. I looked at Kate, who nodded in agreement.

So I took a bite and it tasted wonderful.

After our baskets were full we returned to the barn, which was so nice inside that it could only barely be considered a barn any more. I treated everyone to cider and doughnuts.

After a stop off at home for a quick nap and change of clothes it we were off to church. It was a busy day, but I had to admit that the idea of moving here was gaining traction in my heart. As we drove along the highway, Martin pointed out the church.

"Behind the mall?" I asked.

Martin laughed, "No, that mall *is* the church."

I can, with complete honesty, say that I had never seen anything like it before. The parking lot along was bigger than anything I would have thought real. It was bigger than Meijer or Walmart. The only thing that might have come close is the ballpark. There were people directing traffic. A girl, who looked fourteen offered me a ride to in a golf cart—*to the front door!*

Once we were inside, while Martin and Kate went to drop Kristen at the childcare center, the boys pulled me to their designated area. The place looked more like a bar or a rec room than a church. There were couches, Ping-Pong and foosball tables, and a stage that reminded me of the time I went to see Paul Simon in concert. Yet, however strange, it was clear that the boys were excited to be there, and so engaged with both the adults and the other kids. I had to pull myself away, not because really I wanted to stay, but because there was something intoxicating about all that energy in a church.

I wandered back toward the entrance but did not immediately find Kate or Martin. But as I waited, several people welcomed me and asked me if I was new. Eventually I found Martin and we sat down. Kate joined us a minute later, waving to several people as she did. When the service began I was without words. I had attended the same church for the last thirty-five years. In that time we had added the occasional guitar or special music sung to a track, but I was not prepared for the semi-professional musicians on stage: guitar, bass, trumpet, a choir, soloists, and drums tucked behind some kind of bulletproof shield.

At first I was hesitant because it didn't fit with what I understood church to be, but then, over the next twenty minutes, as I sang along with songs I did not know and clapped my hands when I couldn't find the melody, wave after wave of warm emotion swept through me. People raised their hands and closed their eyes and were so…vulnerable. I looked over at Martin and Kate, trying not to make them feel self-conscious. It moved me to see my child, grown, and worshipping with such passion.

As I sat down, and as the musicians cleared the stage, I thought, *How could I return to a life without this? How could I return to my own church after this? What I had wasn't just dull, it seemed passionless, pointless.*

The preacher walked on stage. He wore a suit, but immediately took off his jacket and rolled up his sleeves, which bothered me for some reason. Why wouldn't he just wear short sleeves? But I decided I was being picky. He walked around the stage with confidence, his hair bobbing for a second after he stopped walking. My ears were still ringing a little from the music, so I must have missed the scripture reading for the day.

"We live in a world that only focuses on itself. Look in the newspaper, on television, in magazines and what do you see? There is world that is full of drugs, and gangs, and crime and war and hate. We are living in a time of moral bankruptcy. Everywhere you look there are signs that things are not the way God intended them to be. I read that witchcraft is even becoming popular again. With our children. In our schools. It's a shame."

Kristen was nodding her head. Martin was twisting his wedding ring around his hand. The preacher continued, "But as Christians we are called to a different life. A life of service. A life of putting other people before ourselves. The world tells us to follow our gut, but Christ says, 'Follow me.' We need to stand up to the world and say that we are Christians and we have a truth that we want to share with you."

Several people near the front stood up and clapped at this.

"You might be sitting there thinking about a situation at work or at home—a situation where you don't know what to do. But you *know* what to do. The Holy Spirit is moving in this place. The Holy Spirit is moving in your hearts. You *know* what to do. Put Christ first, other people second, and yourself third. That might sound easy, but it's hard to do. The world says we should work hard, make money, get stuff. But if we lose it all, what's the point? If we abandon our family, what good are our accomplishments? Paul's letter to the Corinthians says, I can have everything, but if I have not love, I am nothing. If you have everything you want, but don't have the love of Christ and the fellowship of believers. You have nothing. If you go after what *you* want and abandon the family that God has given you, then you are going to outside his will for your life."

Kate shifted in her seat next to me and something tensed within me, like a turtle pulling into its shell.

The preacher lowered his voice, which raised the intensity. "I know the pull of the world. I can't lie and say that I don't. But I also know that it is false. It is a lie. The purpose of our life isn't to follow our own hearts. It is to follow God's heart. It is to do what *God* wants."

He went on like this for a while longer, but I had stopped listening. The service ended with a song that I would have found very moving thirty minutes ago, but which now felt a little contrived.

When we got outside it felt like coming out of a movie theater, a return to a reality that is not as vibrant or sexy. I didn't say much on the ride home. By the time we arrived back at the house, the sun had set. Kate began making dinner. She really did have a beautiful house, a wonderful husband, and great kids. I would probably be happy living in her guestroom.

I went upstairs and began packing my things.

The more I drove through Pittsburgh the more lost I became. Three times I went over a bridge and ended up heading out of the city. I turned my car around to head back into the city only to realize several minutes later that I was now on a different bridge altogether and was once again, heading out of the city. What was most frustrating was that I could *see* downtown as I drove—all its tall buildings, glass exteriors, and many windows—I could see where I wanted to be, but I just didn't know how to get there.

It was no better on side streets. They twisted and stuck to my car. I ran into several dead-ends and had to back out under the eyes of people who seemed to have nothing better to do than watch me. But then, I saw my oasis in the urban desert: a Rite-Aid drugstore.

Once I was inside I could have been back in my local Rite-Aid. There was the same layout, the same harsh lighting, and the same smell of unopened Juicy Fruit. I wandered the aisles, past the greeting cards, through the pharmaceuticals, hair care, and cosmetics. Eventually, I picked up a bottle of orange juice, a packet of peanut M&M's, and a bottle of wine that I decided would make a nice gift to Maggie, if I ever found her apartment. Walking to the checkout I noticed that all the school supplies had been discounted by 50%. I picked up a green spiral bound notebook and a packet of pencils.

I could not tell the ethnicity of the woman who rang up my purchases, but it didn't matter because more than anything else, she was young. Lately everyone's primary characteristic seemed to be that they were young. Not just younger than me, but essentially young. I asked for directions to Lawrenceville and she smiled and said, "You aren't far really. It's going to be ok. You need to head a few blocks east and take a left at the fried chicken place. You'll see a big red rooster out front. Follow the way it's pointing. Then take that road about a mile or two. It all kind of blends together. You never really arrive, so you have to keep your eyes open for what you're looking for. Otherwise you'll miss it."

Twenty minutes later I was looking for parking spot close to my second daughter's apartment. I had to walk four uncertain blocks to the address Kate had written on a slip of paper for me, but it was only when I saw my own last name on the buzzer that I relaxed.

I pressed the buzzer.

I pressed it again.

I pressed it a third time.

"What?" A man's voice.

"Hello?" I said, "Is Maggie there?"

"What do you want?"

"I want to talk to Maggie."

"Brad? Is that you? Maggie doesn't want to talk to you. You need to leave her alone."

"This is not Brad. This is Maggie's father."

"Shit. Sorry man." Silence. Then Maggie's voice.

"Dad? Is that you? I'll be right down." Then quieter and to whomever she was with, "Well, then put your pants on."

A minute later she was pulling me into the apartment. "Oh my goodness I cannot believe that you're here. What are you doing here?"

She sounded so much like Evelyn. I hadn't heard that voice in eight months. It was an alto register with the slightest grovel when she became tired. She looked like me: rounder nose and jawline. Yet, her personality was all her own. Artistic since childhood, she had been living in Pittsburgh for the last two years, but before that it was Denver, Miami, Guam, and Sacramento. Some of the travel was to art schools, some the quest for inspiration, and some were just her flights of fancy.

"Did Kate call? I asked her not to." I said.

Maggie looked at the floor. She'd always been a bad liar. "Um, she told me not to tell you, but, yeah, she called."

"So you know what I'm doing here?"

"Sort of. Kate went on about a typewriter and how you were going to move to Lansing. I didn't understand what she was talking about. You know how her voice goes all high and squeaky when she gets worked up. Anyway, I would rather hear it from you."

Maggie's apartment was a large loft. It was a single, large room divided into sections by the furniture. There was an area for a bed, a kitchen, a living room. At least that was the idea. The way Maggie lived each section blended together.

155

A man came out of the only door in the room: the bathroom.

"Come here," Maggie motioned, "Come and meet my dad. Dad, this is Devon. I was painting Devon when you arrived."

"Without pants?" I asked.

Both of them looked at the floor. But I laughed. "You're adults. I'm not here to tell you what to do."

Maggie bounced back to herself, "Let's sit down and talk about why you are here. Do you want some tea? Devon brought over some excellent green tea."

I had never had *green* tea before—never actually knew there was such a thing—and I couldn't remember the last time I had had *any* tea, but I said I would try some.

As Devon filled a kettle with water, I told the story of what was happening, starting back at the very beginning with how I had finally gotten my office ready so that I would be able to write. I told about the figuring out which typewriter key was not working. I told about taking the books down off the shelves in order to look behind them. I told them how it felt like my heart left my chest and that I couldn't rest until I found it. And as I told them this they both nodded along as if they knew what I was talking about. As I spoke I felt like a student in the presence of much older and wiser teachers. I told them how Kate had taken me to their church and how she had offered that I could stay with her.

The tea smelled good. Devon placed three mismatched mugs on the table.

Maggie asked, "So are you going to do it? Are you going to move to Lansing?"

"I'm not sure. When I was there I thought I would, but now that I've gotten a little distance, I don't know."

Maggie's body relaxed, "Oh, good. Dad, you are *not* an old doddering man. Sometimes Kate treats you like you're ready for the home. You clearly have a lot to give to the world. Even the story you just told proves that you got an ability to tell a good tale. You definitely *should* be writing. I've always thought so. And not just as a hobby—as just something to fill your time in retirement—but because the world needs to hear what you have to say."

I felt my chest expand even as I knew it was an overly generous compliment of a loving daughter to her father. But this is why I loved Maggie so much. She had such an open and giving spirit.

"So you don't think I'm being foolish? Going all the way to New York for a piece I could have gotten cheaper and easier by picking up the phone?"

"No!" Maggie said, "Like you said, you're following your heart. It takes people years to get over their fear and apprehension and figure out what they are supposed to be doing."

Devon nodded, "It's true. Each of us have a unique voice that we need to gift to the world. Most of the time we let worry, responsibility, and other people's opinion stomp us down."

I shrugged, "I feel like I have been one of those people. I've worked my whole life in order to provide for my family, but what I really wish I could be doing—could have done more of—was write."

Devon set his tea down, "But that's great! I mean, most people never figure out what they want to do. They just follow the script. They get good grades in school so they can get into a good college. They do well in college so they can get a good job. They work at their job so they can retire. What you're doing doesn't sound any crazier than that. What does it all mean if you can't follow the call of your heart? Going after this piece to fix your typewrite doesn't seem crazier to me than *not* going. Or working a job you hate. Or staying with someone you don't love. And people do those things all the time. Crazy is as crazy does."

How was this barefoot young man making so much sense? I wondered if Evelyn ever felt this way. Over the years we would talk occasionally about my writing, about how I wished I had more time, but how life always seemed to get in the way. She was supportive, but not forceful. Maybe if she had *insisted* I write then I would have...

"Oh!" Maggie said, "What time is it?"

I looked at my watch, "8:30."

"We're late. We are going to meet people at Antonio's. It's the weekly gathering of our artist's collective. Will you come?"

"Will there be food? I haven't had much to eat today."

After assurances that there would be "a-ma-zing" food, and after spending what felt like far too much time searching for Maggie's misplaced sketchbook, we loaded into my car. This gave me a few minutes to ask Devon some questions.

Twenty minutes later we arrived at Antonio's and were shown to a semi-private section in the back. I met the gang. There was Peter, who had a mustache and taught French at the University. Next to him was Marcus, a sculptor who called Devon his cousin, but in a way that made me wonder what exactly the word meant. There was Marie and Beth, tattooed and pierced and sitting close to one another. When I shook their hands all they said were "poet" and "muse" respectively. Devon went to the other side of the table, to man whose name I did not catch, and joined a loud, academic argument. I sat down to a woman who Maggie introduced as Beatrice.

"Call me B."

We shook hands. She was probably only a couple years younger than I, which immediately made her the most interesting person at the table. She has also draped in a deep beauty that only women after a certain age can wear.

Conversation was fast and fluid. I didn't know much about what they were talking about but I tried to pick up pieces, not so that I could participate, but because it all seemed so energizing. There was talk of Martha Nussbaum, Jacques Derrida, and Picasso, spliced with conversation about Nirvana, Seinfeld, and Reagan's effect on the working class. The whole time, the conversation would bubble across the table for a while and then B would make a comment, which everyone paid attention to, and that inevitably sent the talk scrambling off in a new direction.

The Sangria was making me warm, but I was also a little tipsy from the conversation. I had never been with a group of people who took art, politics, and life so seriously. The talk, the wine, the people, they all gave me a sense of potential—that a person could make a difference, not only in how they voted, but in the art they made, how they dressed, slept, ate, watched or listened to; there was no part of life that did not seem to matter to these people.

I felt a tap on my shoulder. Beatrice whispered in my ear, "Smoke?"

I looked at her.

"Come on. Walk me outside."

I followed her.

Outside the restaurant the sound dropped away. B lit a cigarette and offered me one. I almost took one, even though I didn't smoke, but I decided it would be less cool to take one, cough up a storm, and *prove* I had no idea how to smoke. But Beatrice didn't mind. She took a long drag and looked me up and down.

"How old are you?"

I told her.

"I like you."

I was startled by her directness, "You don't know me." I said.

"Do I need to? Why can't I like you? You interest me." She pointed toward the door. "You aren't like them. You're…"

"Old?"

She smiled, "Seasoned. Experienced. Deeper. Walk with me. I won't take you too far. They'll go on and on like that for hours if I let them. They talk about themselves and their struggles as if they are unique. They haven't lived long enough to realize they aren't original. Give them ten or fifteen years. Give them divorce, abortions, skin cancer, a child, or a dying parent."

I stopped walking.

"Sorry, good example. Poor timing. Maggie kept us informed as everything was happening with your wife."

We started to walk again.

"You don't like the conversation in there?" I asked.

"Oh, it's wonderful. But its just talk. I've been having conversations like that since I was their age. They are all good people, several of them have a lot of undeveloped potential, your Maggie included. But sometimes I tire of being seen as the *grande dame* of creativity and artistry."

"What are you talking about?" I asked.

She stopped walking and looked at me. Then she laughed, "It is wonderful to meet someone who has no idea who I am. Genuinely no idea." She took my hand and we walked hand in hand. Whatever it was: the wine, the smoke, the conversation, or the touch of this enchanting woman, I went with it. We were just holding hands after all. Just as there needed to be more words for "tired" there needed to be a word for what I was feeling.

For a block we said nothing. B finished her cigarette and stomped it out.

"Are you just here to visit Maggie? Are you going to be here several days?"

I smiled, "Actually this is all kind of a wild, free-flowing trip. I have a general direction where I'm heading, but I'm giving myself to freedom to go where and when I want to. I had hoped to get some writing done."

"You're a writer?"

"Trying to be."

"Interesting."

"Is it?"

Beatrice nodded, "Let me say this, I'm sensitive to the fact that your wife died less than a year ago. But I'm also wondering if you'd like to join me tomorrow. I have a little business to take care of at the Carnegie, but we could meet around 10:30 and you could come with me. We could talk as adults should, during the light of day, rather than all of these children talking in the night."

"Let me talk to Maggie, but I think that should work. I would like that."

"Good." She kissed my cheek and we walked back to the restaurant to rejoin the group.

As I sat there I realized that for the first time in thirty-five years I had a first date.

We got back to Maggie's apartment around 1:00 am. I had lost steam around midnight, around the time B excused herself, but the rest of the group was going strong even as they said goodbye on the street.

Devon went to "crash" with Peter, which was nice because then I didn't have to think about sleeping arrangements. I told Maggie that enjoyed the conversation and I asked her questions about the people. Maggie told me about an idea she and one of the tattooed girls had for a joint project. When she asked about my walk with B and I told her about my plans for the next day. She was a little surprised, but said, "That's good I guess. I have to work anyway."

Back at the apartment I thought I would fall immediately to sleep, but my brain kept spinning. I told Maggie I would sleep on the couch and she didn't protest.

She was snoring within minutes.

I took out my new notebook and one of my pencils and wrote:

I had a great night. The conversation at Antonia's was thought provoking. I don't think I've ever been around people so creative. I didn't understand half of what they were talking about, but there was rawness and an energy that I could almost feel. Beatrice is something altogether different. She leaves me feeling something—like I need to gulp her down. That sounds strange even as I write it.

My pencil broke, so I grabbed a pen that Maggie had left on the end table and continued writing.

But I had such a wonderful time. I feel a little buzzed, but I don't think it's from the wine. I think it's from finding a community of people who are willing to take risks, take art seriously, and encourage one another to pursue their projects, even when they don't make sense. Maybe I should join this group. I've never been one for city life, but if I felt this way all the time I might consider it. B? What about B?

I only wish I could be writing more. That's one thing I haven't done enough of on this trip. But I guess that's why I'm taking this trip, so that I can write. I've been so busy that I just haven't had the time. I suppose this counts, but it doesn't feel like it does. I'm not going to sleep anytime soon.

I wrote until the darkest hour of the night. Only then did I fall asleep for a couple of hours, until Maggie's alarm woke us both.

Over toast, I began to wonder if Maggie wasn't entirely comfortable with my plans for the day. When she came out of the bathroom in her bright blue

Magic Smile Teeth Whitening polo shirt and black pants I asked her how she was doing.

"Fine." Was all she said, but I guessed that while she was fine bringing her dad to her meeting, to show him how amazing her friends were, how good her life was; that it made her uncomfortable that he was lingering, leaving fingerprints on her world. Or was there something more?

I met B on the steps of the Carnegie Museum of Art around mid-morning. It was a clear day and I had walked instead of driven, which made me a few minutes late. B was waiting and gave me a wave when she saw me. She actually looked relieved, as if she was worried that I might not show up. We went inside together and she took me past the guards and the ticketing agents. I figured at the time that that she must have had an annual membership.

"Follow me." she smiled, "I want to show you something."

We walked together, away from the crowd, toward a section of the museum that was cordoned off behind temporary walls. But B lifted a velvet rope and directed me inside. A gentleman wearing a bow tie and showing a lot of cuff out of his suit coat kissed B on both cheeks. B introduced me and we shook hands. She told me the two of them had a few things to discuss and asked if I would look around the room. She said that she would be curious what I thought.

The room was circular, so I started to the right, leaving Beatrice and the bow tie in the center of the room. I had already made it about a third of the way around the room, and I still hadn't thought of anything clever to say to B about what I was looking at.

164

Then I saw it. It was a painting of a red bird in a cage: its mouth wide open in protest, but the cage door also wide open. It was my bird. I knew that it was the same bird in the same way you know that your heartbeat is your heartbeat.

"What do you think?"

I startled.

"Sorry," B interlocked her arm into mine, "I didn't mean to frighten you."

"No, it's ok." I said, "This one. There's something about it."

"Do you like it?"

"I think so. I mean…it's great. I'm just feeling a couple of different things right now. Who is the artist?"

B gave me a strange look and then started laughing. "Well, *me*! I thought you knew that." She covered her mouth in embarrassment, not for her art, but for my stupidity. She chuckled for a little while longer, but I didn't even mind.

"Well, then it's spectacular. They're all spectacular."

"Be honest."

"So you're a big deal?"

"Not to you, obviously."

"But to people who know about this stuff."

"There's always someone bigger, better."

"But you're important enough to have a show."

She nodded.

We spent the next forty minutes walking around the room, but I never stopped knowing exactly where the painting of the bird was. Even when I wasn't looking at it, I could feel it watching me. B explained a lot of things about each piece that I did not understand, but I wanted to. It was different than last night and I didn't think it was just the time of day. She spoke with authority, layering unsaid things in between all the things she was saying, anticipating my questions because she had already asked them herself.

"So," I asked, "What do *you* think of this?" I motioned around the room when we returned to where we entered.

She sighed, "I'm afraid I'm repeating myself."

"Well, I don't know your earlier work, so I can't speak to that. But I can tell you that I think it's a great show, collection, whatever you call it. Are you nervous they won't sell?"

"It's not like that. It's not a gallery. Most of them are already owned by other people. The collection is pulled together by the museum."

"Sorry," I said, "I really have no idea how all this works."

I was suddenly very thirsty. B said that there was much more to see in the Museum and that she hadn't intended that the whole visit would be spent on her pieces, but I said that I didn't mind just seeing her, that it was it was more art that I usually saw in a year. The truth was, that the show had been so intimate and personal and vulnerable that I needed a break.

We walked three blocks to a coffee shop. I was amazed how comfortable I felt with her. It was then I realized that maybe the reason Maggie had acted so strange was the idea of her father, recently widowed, spending time with another woman.

I let B order for us and she came back with two lemonades, which blew me away. I had never met a woman with the confidence to order for someone. I started talking about Evelyn and the typewriter. I told her that I felt a little crazy and very much alive. I told her about writing books and about how the life I had lived had not prepared me to write, but that I still wanted to do it anyway. She told me about marrying too young, about her divorce that waited too long, and how now it was almost 15 years of living on her own. She spoke more about her fears of her upcoming show and I told her about my big fear of dying and the even bigger fear of living and being happy again.

We ordered lunch.

"Tell me about the painting of the red bird." I asked.

"It began as just an exercise. It was never meant to become anything. One day the most beautiful red bird landed outside my window. I have very little interest in birds, but this one was so stunning that I stopped what I was doing. I wish I could explain it better. It was like the sum of all red birds that have ever lived. What bird could be that red and not be caught by some predator? It sat on my sill for a long time. Then it sat in my mind for much longer. The only way I could get it out was to paint it."

"Amazing." I said, "It was my favorite. I can't stop thinking about it."

B softened all across her face and shoulders. She looked out the window, "How long are you going to stay in Pittsburgh?"

Many hours later I arrived back at Maggie's apartment.

Maggie was not home yet, but would be soon. I wandered the apartment, stepping around canvases and art books and clothes. I could not see myself living here, not like this, not the way I could see myself living at Kate's. I mean, I couldn't move in with Maggie. But there were things I liked about the city. B had invited me to stay as long as I wanted. She had tempted me by offering, "You could work on your book in the morning and we could visit museums together in the afternoon. Or just walk the city. There are always things going on at the University. You would be close to Maggie. You would be immediately plugged into the creative community here."

It was an idea that I found desirable. But as I looked around Maggie's apartment I had a vision of her room as a teenager: strewn clothes, art books, CD cases, jewelry, papers. It was as if I was seeing both rooms at the same time. And to those overlaid visions came a third vision of B's painting. The three images confused me. I closed my eyes, but this only made things worse. I ran to the sink and drank a glass of water, which seemed to help clear my head.

Then, clarity.

I wrote two notes. I taped one closed and wrote "B" on the outside. The other I wrote "Maggie" on and added $20. I placed both notes on the kitchen table where Maggie would see them. Then I quickly packed my bags and left before she got home.

I drove around the block six times before a parking spot opened up close to Esther's apartment. On the final time around the block Esther was sitting on the steps and we waved to each other. Then, to my great luck, a car pulled out only six or seven cars ahead of me. Esther ran over and gave me a big hug.

"Kate called to tell me that you might be coming my way, but she never told me when you would be here. Then Maggie called this morning on the edge of tears, telling me that you have vanished from her apartment."

"Yeah," I said, "I suppose I've been a little more erratic lately than everyone would like me to be." I shrugged, "Maybe I'm testing my retirement wings. I figure I can float along with the breeze. Driving here I did wonder if I'm putting you girls out. Maybe I should have called sooner. I'll try to be better." I rocked back and forth on the balls of my feet, my hands clasped behind my back, not fully believing what I was saying.

Esther gave my arm a squeeze, "Come on in. You have got to be tired. You can meet some of my housemates."

Esther shared a townhouse with six other people. Everyone had their own room, but they shared living spaces, bathrooms, kitchen, and household duties. The idea was that they shared everything in common which would make it possible to afford to live in New York and not work for a hedge fund. I had been here once before when I traveled to Albany and I can honestly say that I liked the people Esther lived with, they were practical, hardworking people who knew that it was impossible to get by in New York, or in the world for that matter, on your own. A couple of faces had changed since my last visit, but the stories were basically the same. There were two medical students, a sound-engineer from a local radio station, two people I can't remember, and another girl who worked with Esther at the clinic. It was packed tight, but it was clean and people were kind.

I had driven through the night, stopping for a couple hours sleep at a rest area, so it was only mid-morning. Esther introduced me to people in various states of readiness: finishing breakfast, pouring coffee, discussing shower schedules. She offered me coffee and asked if I wanted a scone. I had no idea what a scone was, so I kept with the coffee. We sat down at the dining room table and the others continued with their morning rituals.

"So, how *are* you?" Esther smiled at me.

"I'm good. What did Kate tell you? Or Maggie? I should really call Maggie and let her know that I'm ok. I did leave her a note."

Esther smiled again, "Ah, well, you know Kate. She says a lot. And Maggie mentioned the note, but was pretty dramatic about how you cut out of there."

"I left a note."

"She found it eventually, just not right away."

"I put it on the kitchen table."

"Maggie couldn't find her nose."

A laugh bubbled up inside both of us when Esther said this because it was a phrase that was a favorite of Evelyn's—but the bubbles popped as smiles.

Esther continued, "They'll be fine. I wanted to hear what *you* had to say and what brought you out to New York. I hear there's something about a typewriter."

Esther always had a way of drawing me out. I think it was because I had the easiest time seeing her as an adult. Even as a little girl she rarely acted like she needed any kind of protecting or providing. She took care of her own skinned knees, bad teachers, and heartbreak. We are, of course, a combination of all our past selves—who we were as a child, a teenager, a young person—but Esther has been a consistent person most of her life. She had always been who she always is.

"Well, I'm not sure I want to tell the story...." I began.

"What is it?" Esther asked.

"Well, it's just that I'm not sure I want to tell you." I said, "The more I talk about the more silly it seems. I've told it to Kate and then to Maggie. And I'm sure they've told it to you. But each time I tell it, it seems crazier and crazier to me. I'm afraid that if I tell it too much then it's going to seem so crazy that I'll stop."

Esther nodded, "But, dad, doesn't that tell you something? Doesn't it tell you something about what you're trying to do if, every time you talk about it, it becomes less sensible?"

I looked into my cup. I knew she was right, but I also knew she was talking the way she talks to people at the clinic—using her social work voice. There were coffee grounds sticking to the sides and bottom of my mug.

"I know. Right? But at the same time I can't stop. I'm compelled. I'm not sure what it is, but I've got to see this thing through. The shortest version of the story is that my typewriter broke and I'm traveling to the factory to get a replacement part. I know it would be easier to make a phone call. But I'm doing this."

Esther nodded, "Kate thinks this is all about Mom; that you're taking this trip as a way to deal with your grief. Maggie said that she thinks you're trying to discover your true self, your inner child or something like that."

I nodded, "I'm not so arrogant as to believe those aren't factors. Of course I would never have done this if Mom hadn't died. Can you imagine her letting me go off like this? It's all part of the equation, but the thing I'm realizing is that there *is* no equation. There is no formula where you put in the hard work and sacrifice on one side and get happiness and old age on the other. Your mother was part of everything I did for so long that she's still part of everything I do, even if she isn't around anymore. And Maggie is right too. I do need to figure out what the future is going to bring. But while both of them are right, they are both also wrong. This trip is not about your mother, not even about me, but it's about…well, I suppose it's about trying to figure out what it's all about."

Esther slapped her thighs, "Ok. I'm glad we figured out all you're doing is trying to discover the meaning of life. And we can talk more about this, but right now, I'm late for work."

"Oh," I looked at my watch, "I'm sorry about that. Um, is there anything I can do, like volunteer-wise?"

"I was hoping you would offer. Otherwise I was going to have to conscript you."

Esther was only twenty-eight years old but was already the Assistant Director of the New Hope Help Center: a three-story building that held transitional housing, a medical clinic, offered job training, and, on the main floor served lunch to over 400 people, seven days a week. She had a heart that always looked outward. As a kid she had taken care of sick animals she found and had stopped eating meat long before it became popular to do so.

At the Center, she gave me a tour, which really was impressive, not in the way that a factory or office building is impressive, but impressive in its utility. It was not a large building, but every space was used. I had a lot of questions about their funding sources and the extent of the medical services they were able to offer the community, but there wasn't time for detailed answers. Like a kid at daycare, she dropped me off at the kitchen. It was a place of polished steel and oversized pots and long-handled serving spoons. Here I met Roxanne, who was happy in an aggressive way that let you knew as long as you followed her directions you would be best friends, but if you stepped out, she would step up. She put me to work chopping onions into small pieces that would be sautéed.

Roxanne explained, "We've having omelets today. It's something we do once in a while because it's a lot of work. People love it when we do."

Once I had diced six onions, I asked what else he could do, assuming that it would be enough. Roxanne just laughed, "Oh, honey. You got to keep on chopping till you weep." Soon other people joined the crew and began cracking eggs, cutting potatoes, slicing into peppers, and frying up bacon and sausage. I was swept up on the energy that was building as people shouted out how many minutes before 11:30 it was. "10 left." What seemed like seconds later, Roxanne shouted, "5 left." I worked steadily, but no sooner had I built up a nice stockpile of onions than they were whisked away to a hot skillet. The place began to smell alive.

Then the doors opened.

I had expected a mad rush of hungry people to scramble through the door. And there were a few who hustled to the front of the line, but mostly people were polite, quiet, and orderly. Roxanne switched me to pouring juice, advising me to give everyone just one cup, even if they asked for more. My eyes were still dripping from all the onions, and they continued to be wet long after they should have dried.

I saw men my own age, women younger than my girls, and families, *families!* with young children. I filled their cups to the top. I saw veterans of three different military conflicts. Young men, barely out of boyhood, in hooded sweatshirts and shifty eyes, but who politely thanked each of us on the line. I saw people eating alone, or making conversation with strangers, and still others who seemed to know each other quite well. The servers moved among one another with purpose and grace. When they ran out of diced potatoes they apologized and switched to offering cereal. No one complained. People were offering what they had and taking what they got. Even when my forearm began to ache and cramp because I couldn't pour accurately with my left hand, I kept on. I was part of something. Something real. Something that felt good.

The ninety minutes for lunch service went by before I could blink. When they closed down the crew made plates for themselves from whatever was left over and I joined them in the kitchen, very hungry myself. It is not an exaggeration to say that it was some of the best food I have ever tasted. The crew told stories as they ate and there was laughter and I felt very much a part of things. But soon, without a word, everyone shifted to cleaning up. The kitchen steamed up as the industrial washer began to work overtime on the plates and silverware and glasses. I was assigned to scrub the biggest pots because I had the longest arms. I turned on the sprayer too hard and the water hit the bottom of the pots and splashed back all over my face, covering me in suds and laughter.

Once everything was cleaned up I sat down with a cup of coffee in the empty dining room. The sun was shining in the windows and its warmth was welcome but unnecessary because I felt warm within. I had spent so much of the last year stuck in my own head that I had forgotten that there were other people with bigger problems in the world. This life—both of the homeless people I was serving and of the workers offering the food—was so different than anything I experienced in my daily life that I was a little disoriented.

I got out my notebook and wrote:

Why was I so worried about getting a silly key for a silly machine to write a novel that no one might ever read? When there are people who need something as basic as food, who am I to spend my time writing? Does the world really need what I have to say? Does the world really need another novel by a white male who is soon to be in his sixties? What do I have to add? What do I have that is more important than helping to relieve just a little bit of the suffering of the people around me? And there is so much that needs to be done. The clinic only serves lunch, so where do these people go for breakfast or for dinner? Are the kids in school? There is so much that I don't understand. And of course I wouldn't have to do this in New York. I assume there are people who need help near home. Or in Lansing. Or in Pittsburgh. Maybe? I'm sure it's somewhere if I dug a little deeper. Though nothing like this. I've never experienced anything like this.

Esther found me staring out the window.

"Are you ok?" She asked.

"Oh, I'm wonderful. It is clearly such a good thing you're doing here. Obviously I don't need to tell you how much work it is."

"Roxanne said you were a natural, chatting up people as they came through the line."

"Oh, really? I felt like I never knew what to say."

Esther motioned for me to follow her back to her office. As we walked together she explained, "There's a lot of heartbreak in this job, but we do a lot of good too. Sometimes I get frustrated that the government programs don't seem to address long-term problems, but on the other hand, any assistance we can get is welcome. It's always hard to keep our doors open. Our Director spends most of his time traveling around trying to secure funding, which means that most of the operational tasks fall to me. But we've got a good team of people here. And when things get really tough: when someone OD's or when kids go missing, then I remind myself that if we weren't here they wouldn't have the services they *do* have. I know that at the end of the day I have made the world a better place, and that makes me feel good."

I stopped and looked at my youngest daughter. Here she was, not even thirty years old and so selfless and giving. When I was thirty, my biggest concern had been trying to pay for private school for three girls. I was working long days so that Evelyn could be at home when the girls got home from school.

When we got to Esther's office she had me sit down and she closed the door. There were piles of papers, stacks of first-aid kits, boxes of medical syringes; but even though they seemed disconnected, there was a sense of purpose and neatness in the disorder. She sat at her desk and I got the feeling that this was not the first time she had brought someone in here for a little talk.

Twenty-four hours later I walked into the offices of the Royal Typewriter Company. A wonderfully plump woman sat behind a low desk.

"Can I help you?" she asked.

I held up a finger to ask for a second. I was a little out of breath.

"Yes." I stood up straight and made myself as tall as I could, "I need a replacement arm for a typewriter, one of yours, a Futura 800. My e went missing and I've taken a bit of a drive to get here, and now I'm here and I'm hoping I could get a replacement from you. I need a new e."

The woman gave me a sad smile, "Well, sir?"

"Yes?"

"I wish you had called ahead. I could have saved you some hassle. You're in the right place, in one respect. This *is* the head office for the Royal Typewriter Company. But it's the *sales* offices. All our manufacturing is done in Hartford, Connecticut. If you would have called, we would have been glad to send you the replacement part that you specify, but we don't have spare parts here. Our salesmen, Robert or Peter couldn't even sell you a replacement machine directly. They could take your order, but the machine would still be built and shipped from the Hartford factory. Here, have a seat."

It must have shown on my face that I was feeling a little light-headed because the woman got up from her desk and led me to a seat against the wall.

"Let me get you a glass of water."

She disappeared and returned with a coffee mug full of tap water and a single, lonely ice cube.

I thanked her and asked if I could just sit for a minute. She asked if there was anyone she could call to come and get me and I shook my head no. "The truth," she said, sitting down next to me, "Is that not a lot of people *want* typewriters anymore." She leaned over to me and whispered, "Can you keep a secret?" without waiting for my reply she went on, "The company is shutting down. I'm already working on a position at my cousin's law firm. They've got computers there and typing on one of those is just like typing here." She waved her hand over to her desk. "I know it's odd to say this, seeing how I work here, but typewriters are a thing of the past. You should consider a computer. I know they are ghastly expensive, but they can do a lot of things. I hear."

I thanked her for the water and excused myself. I needed some air. I walked out and the sun was shining so brightly, but I felt so cold. I began to walk back to my car, but when I reached it I just kept walking past it. I just walked and walked, taking lefts or rights for no reason at all beyond chance. I felt like a limp sail on a windless day. I caught my foot on a crack and almost fell into an alleyway, but righted myself in time. A man laughed at me as I stumbled past.

It was at that moment that I finally saw myself through my daughters' eyes. I was an aging man who had lost his wife to cancer and who was trying to figure out life by fixating on this one thing, this one insignificant thing that could easily be fixed with a phone call. What would change when I got back home? Would I be any different? What did having a working typewriter change anything? For that matter, what would writing change? Ev would still be gone and I would still be alone.

I walked on and on, losing my sense of direction and any idea where my car was or how to get back to Esther's apartment. I touched my face and was surprised to find it wet. Was I crying? I found a public park and sat down on the bench. I began to write.

What am I going to do? I am at a dead end. I could go on to the factory, but I see myself and am saddened by what I see. I am a mess of a man. I should go home. I should move to Lansing and spend the rest of my days with Kate. Or I could choose Pittsburgh and Maggie—and B. That wouldn't be bad. Or I could work with Esther at the clinic. I'm not sure I could afford the rent, even with the life insurance money, but they are doing such amazing work there. I need to give up. I'm done. I miss Evelyn and that is all this is about. I need to go home.

I closed the notebook.

I closed my eyes and felt the sun on my face. Somehow hearing was easier than seeing. I listened to the creaking and giggling of a mother pushing her daughter on a swing on. I heard cars and trucks rumbling and honking. Then I heard a single tweet, but I didn't open my eyes. I didn't want to see what I knew I would.

"I'm done following you. You're a wild goose—that is what you are—and you've led me on a wild-goose chase. I hate you. You promise me so much. I believed that you knew where you were leading me. Get out of here. I'm done with you."

I did open my eyes to wave my hand, but the bird didn't leave. It hopped around in a circle, as if it wanted me to follow it.

"No." I said, "I'm not going to follow you any longer. Kate is right, because I taught her well and *I* was right. I've always known this was a stupid idea. Now I'm not going to throw any more time or energy into this. It's stupid. So you can get out of here."

And as if it heard me, it flew away.

I fell into a state of submission. I was caught in the current of sadness, but I was done fighting it. And to my surprise, I felt calm. Numbness was probably as close as I was going to get to feeling some kind of peace.

When I got back to Esther's I was surprised to find Kate and Maggie sitting around the living room.

"Girls!" I exclaimed, "What are you *doing* here?"

Kate looked at her sisters, Esther nodded, but Maggie looked into her hands.

Kate spoke, "We need to talk. But first, did you get what you came for? Esther told me you were on your way to get the replacement part."

I shook my head, "No. It was just the showroom. Turns out that the factory is in Connecticut and it was only a showroom that I visited, a kind of sales office. I can't say I'm thrilled at the prospect of another day of traveling, so…"

Kate interrupted, "No."

"What?" I said.

"You can't go. This has got to end. This is why Maggie and I came all the way out here. We both think that you're not dealing with Mom's death well. This is a crazy quest you're on. You could very easily have gotten what you're looking for without ever leaving your house. Now here you are, a thousand miles from home, and nothing to show for it. What are you going to do if you get to the factory and they don't have the part you need or they don't sell parts directly to the consumer? Have you even thought about that? And now you drag Maggie and me across the country after you…"

It didn't matter that she was right. It didn't matter that she was saying all the things I had just finished thinking, "I didn't ask you to come. I was doing fine. I *am* doing fine."

Esther raised her hand for calm and spoke, "The truth is, Mom's death has been hard on us all. We're not trying to tell you how to live your life, only that all this doesn't seem like you. It isn't who you've been. It's not the person we know."

I turned to Maggie, who still hadn't looked at me, "Do you feel this way too?"

She shrugged "Well, it does seem a little out of character. I love that you're exploring your creative side, but I do wish you had stayed closer to home. You just left without telling me. I was really worried."

I saw just how much I had upset her by how I had left. But how could I have left any other way? If I had stayed a moment more I would have lost my nerve. This whole thing had been dependent on not losing my forward momentum. I needed to keep moving forward. Even this conversation was slowing me down. I needed to drive to Connecticut. How could I still feel the need to go on *and* the desire to submit to their wishes?

"I'm sorry Maggie. I wish I could explain it in a way that you would understand. I really enjoyed Pittsburg, and you have an amazing group of friends, and B was so…kind." Maggie blinked away a few tears, but I continued, "But I needed to do this. I think I still need to do this."

How I loved my daughters. But how could I explain to them what was going on when I didn't fully understand it at the time? What would Evelyn have said? She always seemed to be able to put things in a way that made sense. Or at least that moved things forward. My role had been to drive the car where she wanted to go, grill the meat she chose for the people she invited, to pay for the things she bought. But now? I was looking into three faces filled with fear and who expected answers that I could not give.

"Things were not exactly what I planned." I said.

The girls shared a look, but before any of them could talk I plowed on, "The parts are in a factory. So I'm going to go to the factory."

Kate let out a hot sigh, "Come on Dad. Are you serious? I've got to get home. I've got things I've got to do. You said this would take a week. It's been a week. It's time to go home"

"I never said that. I never said a week. I didn't ask you to come." My voice came out louder than intended.

"Oh, like I should let you go off on your own? You don't even have a suitcase! You have duffle bag like you're some kind of high school kid. You've been running around in the same clothes for a week. What was I supposed to think was happening? Mom died and now my father shows up at my house, unannounced, and tells me that he's going off on a fool's errand that could be easily and more cheaply accomplished with a phone call. So you tell me, did I really have a choice whether to come after you? I just kept thinking of what Mom would say if she knew that I abandoned you."

"Katherine Evelyn Kinde!" I was shouting, but I couldn't stop myself, "You cannot speak to me like that. I am not a child. I know what I am doing. I'm not a senile old man. I have not lost my sense of the world. Don't put that on me. I know what I am doing"

"Then please tell me what the *hell* are you doing? Because I don't understand it. Neither do Maggie or Esther." Kate did not sit down.

"I DON'T KNOW!" I could feel the blood in my face. "BUT I KNOW I'M GOING TO DO IT!"

A crisp silence expanded from my being and pushed back against Kate with a real physicality until she had to leave the room and slam the door to Esther's bedroom. The walls were thin enough that we could all hear her crying. Maggie went immediately after her, but Esther stayed, tracing the grooves of the arm of her chair.

I leaned back. I was afraid that I would never be able to stand up again.

Esther looked directly at me, "It's hard with Mom gone."

I returned her look but didn't say anything.

"You should know that Kate really looks up to you, we all do. We all miss Mom and we need you to be that stabilizing force right now. Everything you're doing, which I think is natural and understandable, well, you're hurting us. Kate most of all because she looks up to you more than Maggie or I. I don't mean that...I mean that from her perspective you are throwing away everything that she has worked so hard to be: responsible, careful, rational."

"I could see that." I smiled at my youngest daughter, "How did you get so wise?"

Esther stood up, "I spent a lot of time with Mom. Now I'm going to go check on Kate." Then she disappeared into the bedroom, leaving me alone.

Maybe they were right. It certainly seemed that I was hurting Kate and probably the other two as well. But what could I do?

I stood up and walked over to the bedroom.

"Kate?" I knocked on the door but did not open it.

"What?" she did not open it either.

"We'll leave first thing tomorrow morning. We can get breakfast on the road. I'm going to bed now."

I went to my small room that was more like a large closet than a real guest room. I turned on the light, shut the door, and unrolled my sleeping bag. I started emptying my bag so that I could repack it for my trip home. In doing so, I took out the pictures that Kristen had made for me. I stared at them for a long time.

Then I flipped through my notebook. I had filled a lot of pages. It was almost ¾ full now. I took out my pen and flipped to the next blank page. Then I began to write.

I wrote about the last few days. I wrote about how it always felt like Evelyn was missing even though it also always felt like she was in the room. I wrote about listening to B talk over lunch. How it was thrilling to think of her but that I also felt guilty being with her. I wrote fast and sloppy. I paused when I heard the girls getting ready for bed, their laughter in the bathroom reminding me of better days—days I had not appreciated as I was living them. When their footsteps ended and I was sure they were asleep I kept writing even when I had nothing to say. I wrote until I found something to say: I was furious at Evelyn for leaving me. How the *hell* was I supposed to go on living? What did she expect was going to happen to me? Of course, I knew that people die, that was a simple fact of life. I knew this. But why me? She would have been much better off if *I* had been the one to get sick. I didn't know how to be a dad *and* a mom to the girls. I didn't even know how to be myself without Evelyn in the room. I was actively messing up things with Kate. And probably with Maggie and Esther too. I was going to drive straight back home, drop Maggie and Kate off at their houses and I would call the Royal Typewriter Co. when he got home and they would send the piece I needed and it would all be back as it was. It made sense.

I shook out my cramping hand and looked at the clock. It was 2:11 in the morning.

There was something deep inside me, something that had always been there, and it felt like it wasn't me, but was controlling me. Was this how addictions felt? Like an itch that must be scratched? I *had* to go. I had to. I had to. It didn't make sense, but I had to. I must.

The air tingled as I closed the notebook. I felt no fatigue. My muscles were springy and my bones were strong. I knew that sleep would not touch me that night, so I carefully and quickly put everything back into my bag. I rolled up the sleeping bag and tied it tight with the strings. Shoes. Keys. Jacket. Light off. Light steps. Out the door. Find the car. Drive. All-night diner. Directions.

Fastest way to Hartford, Connecticut.

5. The Trial of Evelyn

The factory didn't seem to have a main entrance. The only thing that told me I was in the right place was a sign at the road, printed so small that I drove past it and had to turn around. It was an ordinary looking factory—a building like any other. Larger than I expected, but also more run-down, like a ball player past his prime but trying to hang on for one more season. There were a couple of cars parked out front, but I had to climb up the loading dock in order to reach a door that I could knock on.

No one answered.

I opened the door and said, "Hello?"

All I heard was music playing somewhere far away, snaking around many corners and losing volume with each turn, until it reached me, only faint melody and snare drum.

"Hello?" I said as I stepped into the room. There was a greenish tint to everything and it smelled like the frog hut at the zoo. A few pallets of boxes were stacked on the far side of the room and clipboards hung on the wall next to keys and name badges. With no way of knowing where to go and no sign of anyone around, I decided that my best course of action would be to find the source of the music.

This turned out to be harder than I anticipated, as the place was much larger and more complicated than I guessed. Clearly, sections of the building had been added on over the years, resulting in odd junctions and disjointed architecture. This meant that the further I went the more lost I became. I soon wondered if I would be able to find my way out again.

Several times I stopped and listened, but the music never seemed to get any louder. And I never ran into anyone. The place seemed to be living into the predictions of the woman at the sales office: no one wanted a typewriter any more.

After enough time had passed I began to believe that this was more than people late back from a break.

Then a door that I had not noticed before opened.

"Ahhhh!" A woman screamed.

"It's ok. I'm sorry. I didn't mean to surprise you." I held my hands up palms forward.

"You're not supposed to be here!"

"I know. I know. But just give me a chance to explain. I'm not a creep."

"That's what all creeps say."

The woman seemed to quickly get over her initial surprise and find her bearings. She was not a tall woman, nor young. "What are you doing here?" she asked.

"Well, it's a long story." And then I found it hard to know where to begin. Eventually I said, "What happened here? Where is everyone?"

She shrugged, "They're around somewhere. Though there aren't many of us any more. Going to be less real soon. I've got to get back, so you've got to get on with your story.

"I have a Futura 800…"

"Good machine."

"…yes, well, I need an e key. Actually it's the arm that I need."

"Oh, you're looking for a part. Why didn't you say so, follow me. No sense in keeping all the parts around here that we've got. Come on, we've got to head down to the basement."

She lead me back through the door she had come thought and we descended a series of steps into a basement that was even more labyrinthine than the main level. Now I was completely mixed up.

"Happens a couple times a year. Someone like yourself has an attachment to one of our machines and can't move on when it breaks." She pulled open a large sliding industrial door. "We used to be able service all the machines we made, but now, we're going the way of all things I guess. You said a Futura 800?"

"That's right."

We passed by bins of parts stacked deep on shelves.

"That's one of our best, I'm surprised it broke."

"I was surprised myself. I had planned on using it for a long time to come, but then one day I go to write something and *bam*, it's broken! Well, how am I supposed to do what I need to do without an e?"

She nodded, but didn't say anything.

She stopped in front of a bin and let out a large sigh. As she did, it was as if all the sound dropped to the floor and it was just the two of us in that moment.

"What do you need?"

"I need a new e"

"You're sure?"

"Um…yes."

Another sigh. She didn't move.

Then she was flipping through my notebook, but I had no memory of giving it to her. "There's a lot of good stuff in here." How had she gotten it? But I didn't make a move to snatch it back.

She looked at me.

"Can I give you a piece of advice?"

"Ok."

"Just pay attention. Look around at what is happening. Right here, right now, regardless of when it is, and where you are. If you don't, then you aren't going to be able to do anything, much less write. I know it sounds trite, but you can't live in the past or worry about the future. It's not all going to be ok, but worrying it over in your mind isn't going to change anything."

She reached into a bin and selected a key as if it were a flower stem, rather than a piece of steel. "Here you go."

As the key touched my hand the sound returned to the room and the notebook was once again in my bag. I turned it over and saw the two e's, lowercase above uppercase. I look at my guide, who said, "I've got some work to do. Are you going to be able to find your way out?"

I nodded and then I left with exactly what I came for.

6. Denouement

I had already been writing for two hours when the sun rose over Green Lake. I had filled four sheets of lined paper and had to change pens. I had no patience for dying pens. My typewriter looked down on me from on top of the filing cabinet. I wrote longhand. If I thought anything was good enough to develop further, I would rewrite it and send it off to Kate, who had become my unofficial typist and first editor. She was quite the critical eye and oddly, since being included in my process, very encouraging.

Kate and the family were visiting for a few days, which is why I was not surprised when Kristen appeared at my door, blanket in hand and hair poking up at mysterious angles. It had become a bit of a routine between us. She would wake early and come and find me.

"Good morning." I said.

She crawled up on my lap and I covered her with her blanket. A few minutes later Kate appeared, "Kristen, Grandpa's writing, let's not bother him."

Kristen snuggled down under the blanket and ignored her mother.

"Oh, it's ok." I said. "I can write later." Kate looked half a sleep.

"Really." I insisted. "Go back to bed. Enjoy yourself. This is supposed to be vacation for you."

Kristen and I watched the sun rise and burn off the darkness bit by bit.

In a few days, Maggie would arrive too, bringing B with her. And for a day we would all be together. Esther was too busy to get away, but I would call her later, even if it were only for five minutes.

I could not tell if Kristen had fallen back asleep because I could not see her eyes without jostling her, but she hadn't moved in a while. I opened my desk drawer and took out the e key. I felt its bumps and ridges with my thumb. I brought it to my nose and smelled its metallic odor. I gave it a kiss and put it back in the drawer.

Outside the window a bird sang.

Bibliography

Bal PM, Veltkamp M, "How Does Fiction Reading Influence Empathy? An Experimental Investigation on the Role of Emotional Transportation," PLoS ONE 8(1): e55341. Doi:10.1371/journal.pone.0055341

Balthasar, Hans Urs von. *Theo-Drama: Theological Dramatic Theory*. Vol. 1, *Prolegomena*. San Francisco: Ignatius Pr, 1988.

Bayles, David, and Ted Orland. *Art and Fear: Observations On the Perils (And Rewards) of Artmaking*. Santa Cruz, CA: Image Continuum Press, 2001.

Beck, Julie. "Life's Stories." *The Atlantic*, Aug 10, 2015. Accessed September 16, 2015.http://www.theatlantic.com/health/archive/2015/08/life-stories-narrative-psychology-redemption-mental-health/400796/.

Book of Church Order, Reformed Church in America, 12

Booker, Christopher. *The Seven Basic Plots: Why We Tell Stories*. New York: Bloomsbury Academic, 2006.

Brinkerhoff, Robert O. *The Success Case Method: Find Out Quickly What's Working and What's Not*. San Francisco, CA: Berrett-Koehler Publishers, 2003.

Brown, Dale. *Conversations with American Writers: the Doubt, the Faith, the In-Between*. Grand Rapids, MI: Wm. B. Eerdmans Publishing Co., 2008.

Brown, W. Dale. *Of Fiction and Faith: Twelve American Writers Talk About Their Vision and Work*. Grand Rapids, MI: Wm. B. Eerdmans Publishing Co., 1997.

Brown, Robert McAfee. *Persuade Us to Rejoice: the Liberating Power of Fiction*. Louisville, KY: Westminster John Knox Press, 1992.

Buechner, Frederick. *Telling the Truth: the Gospel as Tragedy, Comedy, and Fairy Tale*. San Francisco: Harper & Row, 1977.

Burn, Stephen J. "Jonathan Franzen, the Art of Fiction No. 207." *The Paris Review*, Winter 2010. Accessed November 30, 2015. http://www.theparisreview.org/interviews/6054/the-art-of-fiction-no-207-jonathan-franzen.

Botton, Alain de, and John Armstrong. *Art as Therapy*. London: Phaidon Press, 2013.

Ceaser, James W. "The Origins and Character of American Exceptionalism." *American Political Thought: A Journal of Ideas, Institutions, and Culture,* 1 (Spring, 2012): 1-26. Accessed December 11, 2015. http://www.polisci.wisc.edu/uploads/documents/ceaser.pdf.

Cerwinske, Laura. *Writing as a Healing Art: the Transforming Power of Self-Expression*. New York: Perigee Books, 1999.

Comichron. "Comics and Graphic Novel Sales Hit New 20-Year High in 2014." June 30, 2015. Accessed September 16, 2015. http://blog.comichron.com/2015/06/comics-and-graphic-novel-sales-hit-new.html.

Daniel, Patrick. "The Secret to 'serial': An Afternoon with Sarah Koenig." The Huffington Post. April 16, 2015. Accessed September 16, 2015. http://www.huffingtonpost.com/patrick-daniel/the-secret-to-serial-an-a_b_6995606.html.

Dillard, Annie. *The Writing Life*. New York: Harper Perennial, 2013.

Elbow, Peter. *Embracing Contraries*: *Explorations in Learning and Teaching*, New York, Oxford University Press, 1986.

Elbow, Peter. *Writing with Power: Techniques for Mastering the Writing Process*. 2nd ed. New York: Oxford University Press, 1998.

Elbow, Peter. *Writing Without Teachers*. 2nd ed. New York: Oxford University Press, 1998.

Foster, Thomas C. *How to Read Literature Like a Professor: A Lively and Entertaining Guide to Reading Between the Lines,* New York: Harper Perennial, 2003.

Geertz, Clifford. *Interpretation of Cultures*. publication place: BasicBooks, 1973

Gibson, Megan. "E-Books Go Out of Fashion as Book Sales Revive." *Time*, January 9, 2015. Accessed September 16, 2015. http://time.com/3661173/book-sales-increase-ereaders-slump/.

Gonzalez, Justo L. *The Story of Christianity*. Rev. ed. Vol. 1, *The Early Church to the Dawn of the Reformation*. New York: HarperOne, 2010.

Gonzalez, Justo L. *The Story of Christianity*. 2nd ed. Vol. 2, *The Reformation to the Present Day*. Philadelphia, PA: HarperOne, 2010.

Gottschall, Jonathan. *The Storytelling Animal: How Stories Make Us Human*. Boston: Mariner Books, 2013.

Grimm, E. "Christian Stores Report 2.9% Sales Increase." Christian Booksellers Association. May 6, 2014. Christian Booksellers Association. "Christian Stores Report 2.9% Sales Increase." May 6, 2014. Accessed September 16, 2015. http://cbaonline.org/christian-stores-report-2-9-sales-increase/.

Hansen, Ron. *A Stay Against Confusion: Essays on Faith and Fiction*. New York: HarperCollins Publishers, 2001.

Hauerwas, Stanley. *Why Narrative? Readings in Narrative Theology*. Eugene, OR: Wipf & Stock Pub, 1997.

Herring, Laraine. *Writing Begins with Breath: Embodying Your Authentic Voice*. Boston: Shambhala Publications, Inc., 2007.

Heschel, Abraham Joshua. *The Earth is the Lords & The Sabbath*. New York: Harper Torchbooks, 1966.

Heschel, Abraham J. *The Prophets*. New York: Harper Perennial Modern Classics, 2001.

Holberg, Jennifer L. *Shouts and Whispers: Twenty-One Writers Speak About Their Writing and Their Faith*. Grand Rapids, MI: Wm. B. Eerdmans Publishing Co., 2006.

Holmes, Linda. "Television 2015: Is There Really Too Much Tv?" npr.org. August 17, 2015. Accessed November 30, 2015. http://www.npr.org/sections/monkeysee/2015/08/16/432458841/television-2015-is-there-really-too-much-tv.

hooks, bell. *Teaching to Transgress: Education as the Practice of Freedom*. New York: Routledge, 1994.

Jeffrey, David Lyle, and Gregory Maillet. *Christianity and Literature: Philosophical Foundations and Critical Practice (Christian Worldview Integration)*. Downers Grove: IVP Academic, 2011.

Keen, Suzanne. *Empathy and the Novel*. New York: Oxford University Press, 2010.

Lamott, Anne. *Bird by Bird: Some Instructions of Writing and Life*. New York: Anchor Books, 1995.

L'Engle, Madeleine. *Walking On Water: Reflections On Faith and Art*. Colorado Springs, CO: WaterBrook Press, 2001.

Lewis, C. S. *Of Other Worlds: Essays and Stories*. San Diego: Mariner Books, 2002.

Lott, Bret. *Letters & Life: On Being a Writer, On Being a Christian*. Wheaton: Crossway, 2013.

Martel, Yann. "Learning How to Write Well." Youtube. June 10, 2011. Accessed November 30, 2015.https://www.youtube.com/watch?v=IR9Av-TzSV4&feature=youtu.be.

Moschella, Mary Clark. *Ethnography as a Pastoral Practice: an Introduction*. Cleveland, OH: Pilgrim Press, The, 2008.

Nachmanovitch, Stephen. *Free Play: The Power of Improvisation in Life and the Arts*. New York: Jeremy P Tarcher/Perigee Books, 1990.

Nawotka, Edward. "Profits from Christian Books Make Believers of Top Publishers." *Bloomberg News*, July 25, 2006. Accessed September 16, 2015. http://www.bloomberg.com/apps/news?pid=newsarchive&sid=aFZ KuWjSOYmE.

Newberger, Eric C. "Home Computers and Internet Use in the United States: August 2000." *Current Populations Reports*, September 2001. Accessed December 10, 2015.http://www.census.gov/prod/2001pubs/p23-207.pdf.

Noll, Mark A. *A History of Christianity in the United States and Canada*. Grand Rapids, MI: Wm. B. Eerdmans Publishing Co., 1992.

Oates, Joyce Carol. *The Faith of a Writer: Life, Craft, Art*. Reprint ed. publication place: Ecco, 2004.

Oatley, Keith. *Such Stuff as Dreams: the Psychology of Fiction*. Oxford: Wiley, 2011.

O'Brien, Lucy. "The Future of Video Game Storytelling." IGN. January 12, 2014. Accessed September 16, 2015. http://www.ign.com/articles/2014/01/13/the-future-of-video-game-storytelling.

O'Connor, Flannery. *Mystery and Manners: Occasional Prose (FSG Classics)*. NY: Farrar, Straus and Giroux, 1970.

Osmer, Richard R. *Practical Theology: an Introduction*. Grand Rapids, MI: Wm. B. Eerdmans Publishing Co., 2008.

Peers, Lawrence Palmieri. "Recreating Congregational Stories: Insights from Narrative Therapy" *Congregations* 30, no 4 (fall 2005), 16

Pennebaker, James, and Janel D. Seagal. "Forming a Story: The Health Benefits of Narrative."*Journal of Clinical Psychology* 55, no. 4 (1999): 1243-54.

Plimpton, George. "Garrison Keillor, the Art of Humor No. 2." *The Paris Review*, Fall 1995. Accessed November 28, 2015. http://www.theparisreview.org/interviews/1551/the-art-of-humor-no-2-garrison-keillor.

Plimpton, George. "Maya Angelou, the Art of Fiction No. 119." *The Paris Review*, Fall 1990. Accessed September 16, 2015. http://www.theparisreview.org/interviews/2279/the-art-of-fiction-no-119-maya-angelou.

Plimpton, George, and Frank Crowther. "John Steinbeck, the Art of Fiction No. 45 (Continued)." *The Paris Review*, Fall 1975. Accessed November 30, 2015.http://www.theparisreview.org/interviews/4156/the-art-of-fiction-no-45-continued-john-steinbeck

Roth, Robert. *The Theater of God: Story in Christian Doctrines*. Philadelphia: Wipf & Stock Pub, 2004.

Ryken, Leland. *The Christian Imagination: Essays On Literature and the Arts*. Grand Rapids, Mich.: Baker Book House, 1981.

Sayers, Dorothy L. *The Mind of the Maker*. San Francisco: HarperOne, 1987.

Schneider, Pat. *Writing Alone and with Others*. Oxford: Oxford University Press, 2003.

Shaw, Luci. *Breath for the Bones: Art, Imagination, and Spirit: Reflections on Creativity and Faith*. Nashville: Thomas Nelson, 2007.

Shaw, Luci, and editor. *The Swiftly Tilting Worlds of Madeleine L'engle*. Wheaton, IL: Shaw Books, 2000.

Sontag, Susan. "Directions: Write, Read, Rewrite. Repeat Steps 2 and 3 as Needed" *New York Times*, December 18, 2000, accessed July 16, 2015, http://www.nytimes.com/2000/12/18/arts/18SONT.html?pagewanted=1.

Swinton, John, and Harriet Mowatt. *Practical Theology and Qualitative Research*. LONDON: SCM Press, 2006.

Truby, John. *The Anatomy of Story: 22 Steps to Becoming a Master Storyteller*. New York: Faber & Faber, 2008.

Ueland, Brenda. *If You Want to Write: A Book about Art, Independence and Spirit*. St. Paul: Greywolf Press, 1938.

Wikipedia. "List of Novels Based On Video Games." Accessed September 16, 2015.https://en.wikipedia.org/wiki/List_of_novels_based_on_video_games.

Wilder, Amos Niven, "Story and Story-World" *Interpretations* 37, no 4 (1983): 362.

Wright, Vinita Hampton. *The Soul Tells a Story: Engaging Creativity with Spirituality in the Writing Life*. Downers Grove: InterVarsity Press, 2005.

YouTube. "Writers On Writing with Cornel West (Part 1)." November 10, 2010. Accessed September 16, 2015. https://www.youtube.com/watch?v=TiJGCUKW5xk.

Zimmermann, Susan. *Writing to Heal the Soul: Transforming Grief and Loss Through Writing* New York: Three Rivers Press, 2002.

Zylstra, Sarah Eekhoff. "Religious Fiction Sales Nosedive, Non-Fiction Soars." *Christianity Today*, 4/10/2015. Accessed December 10, 2015.http://www.christianitytoday.com/gleanings/2015/april/religious-fiction-sales-nosedive-non-fiction-soars.html.

Printed in Great Britain
by Amazon